Learning, growing in the art
of living alone, discovering new ways to
socialize, exploring relationships in ways
that are richly rewarding—all of these elements are part of—

THE ART OF LIVING SINGLE

MICHAEL BRODER, PH.D.,

a clinical psychologist practicing in Philadelphia,
is a pioneer in research and counseling for divorce
and transition adjustment. He is a popular speaker
and frequent guest on national television and is
host of psychologically oriented call-in programs
on both CBS radio and NBC Talknet. He is president of the Media Psychology Division of the
American Psychological Association.

THE ART OF LIVING SINGLE

MICHAEL BRODER, PH.D.
with Edward B. Claflin

(Published in hardcover as
Living Single After the Sexual Revolution)

AVON BOOKS ◆ NEW YORK

Published in hardcover as *Living Single After the Sexual Revolution*

AVON BOOKS
a division of
The Hearst Corporation
1350 Avenue of the Americas
New York, New York 10019

First Avon Books Printing: May 1990

AVON TRADEMARK REG. U.S. PAT. OFF. AND IN OTHER COUNTRIES, MARCA REGISTRADA, HECHO EN CANADA.

Printed in Canada

UNV   10 9 8 7 6 5 4

To my daughter Joanne

Contents

Acknowledgments

My thanks go out to the team that helped turn what was a dream—this book—into a reality. First to Ed Claflin, my collaborator, for his writing skills; to Eleanor Rawson of Rawson Associates for her editorial contribution; and to Jane Dystel of the Edward J. Acton Agency for her constant support.

I also thank the thousands of therapy clients whom I've seen over the years, who have contributed greatly to my understanding of the issues of single life. I also am grateful to the many thousands of callers whom I have chatted with over the years on my call-in radio programs; their experiences have helped shape much of my thinking about the singles life. A very special thanks goes out to radio station WCAU-AM (CBS, Philadelphia). I am deeply indebted also to America's two largest talk-radio networks—Westwood One/NBC Talknet and ABC Talkradio—for providing me with national audiences that verified the nationwide consistency of the contemporary issues that are treated in this book.

In addition, there are the many, many people I interviewed especially for this book. They included friends, colleagues, and others who made themselves available to discuss issues with which they had struggled and the solutions (both successful and unsuccessful) they had tried. I would like to thank them all.

I am especially grateful to Peg Duko for her assistance in preparing the manuscript; to Bob Madigan of NBC Talknet for his superb insight into the area of money matters relevant to this book; and to Kiki Olson, an expert on travel for singles, for her expertise and help in that topic.

Throughout the years there have been many people that I have looked to as mentors, but no one has influenced my therapeutic approach as much as Dr. Albert Ellis, the founder of Rational Emotive Therapy, the granddaddy of the short-term cognitive-behavioral therapy orientation. It gains in popularity and relevance with every passing day, and is the orientation in which my approach is most deeply rooted.

This work could never have been completed without the support and encouragement of many of my friends, family, and colleagues. It gives me great pleasure to thank you all. The names are too numerous to mention—but you know who you are.

Finally, thanks to my daughter Joanne, who taught me more about single parenting than I could possibly have learned any other way—especially that a child raised by divorced single parents can be as happy and thrive emotionally as well as any child from an intact home.

To the Reader

Living the good singles life is an art of our times. More people than ever before are living single. Some intend to remain single; others will remain single only until they find a relationship. And there are many of us who are not sure what the future holds. Are we single or not? How do we think of ourselves? How do we intend to live our lives?

We don't automatically *know* what to do. After all, it's unlikely that anyone told us we were destined to be single at this time in our lives. We didn't necessarily plan on it. Some of us have been in marriages or relationships very recently. Others of us are currently involved in a relationship in which we *might* end up living together or getting married in the near future. Or perhaps we're not seeking a romantic involvement of any kind right now, though we remain open to the possibility that we have many options.

We are always changing, and as we change, so do our expectations. What seems impossible now may be possible tomorrow. We can choose to live the single life as we are living it today. Or we can tinker with it, improve it, change it, transform it. We can affect the *nature* of our relationships with people—of the same sex and the opposite sex—so that the very *meaning* of singlehood changes for us.

In suggesting these options, I am not proclaiming that they are open to every one. But I do know that our own single lives can gather richness and dimension if we know the possibilities that are open to each of us. We can learn from the experiences of others. We can learn from looking at ourselves and knowing our own needs and requirements better.

Learning, growing, mastering techniques of living alone, discovering new ways to socialize, exploring relationships in ways that are richly rewarding—all of these elements are part of *the art of living single*.

What This Book Can Do for You

This book has a twofold purpose. First of all, I would like to share with you the words and experiences of some of the people who are now living single in America. Some I know personally, others professionally, and still others I have interviewed especially for this book. I have paraphrased people who have called in to my radio show as well as colleagues who are living single or are dealing professionally with people who are single.

As I've talked with these people about single life, they have reminded me again and again just how many *different* ways there are to enjoy the pleasures and cope with the problems of being single. Their words are refreshing, because they know themselves so well. They have thought long and hard about their needs and have come to terms with the different forces pulling at their lives. I hope their voices will come through clearly on these pages, because individually and collectively they have added vastly to my understanding of what it means to be single—and I hope that they can do the same for you.

If the first purpose of this book is to listen to *their* voices, the second is to listen to your own. Karen, whom you will meet later in this book, is a single woman in her early thirties who has been living alone for several years. "You know," she said, "I discovered what everyone had been telling me. *You have to appreciate your time alone.*"

When Karen began living single, the time alone was the time she dreaded. After several years, *that* time has become the time she values most.

What does it take to like yourself so well that you can value the time you have to yourself? How do you reach a level of self-appreciation and self-understanding so that your time alone is one of your most treasured possessions?

A large part of it is getting to know more about yourself and what you want. At a certain point, you realize that being alone does not mean being *without* other people. It means being *with* yourself. To reach that point, you have to like yourself. You have to get along with yourself. You have to appreciate the things that delight you. So, that's the second thing I would like this book to do for you. If you are already at the stage where you truly enjoy being with yourself, by yourself, then this book may take you farther along your road of self-discovery.

Strategies for Singles

The art of living single also means strategizing to make the best of the time you have with others. Some strategies may already be second nature to you. In one of my interviews, I asked a forty-one-year-old professional whom I will call Lillian whether she ever felt intensely lonely—almost to the point of desperation. Her reply: "No. I don't wait for that to happen. If I'm beginning to feel lonely, I pick up the phone. I talk to my friends, and we make plans."

For Lillian, picking up the phone and talking to her friends is a strategy that *works*. Will it work for you? In all probability, yes. But there are different degrees of loneliness, and some people have a greater or lesser ability to communicate well with their friends.

The point is, these strategies are *available*. You will have to decide for yourself whether a strategy that's right for someone else will be right for you. But whatever the case, if you know about these strategies, you have a greater range of choices.

Commit to it—at least long enough to see whether it works. Some strategies may seem artificial to you. Others may involve some risk. But why not try? You can always drop a strategy if it's not working for you. And consider the benefits: if you try a strategy and it does work, you have just increased your range of choices and your ability to enjoy the singles life.

Also, the strategies that *do* work may become second nature after a while. It's only the first few steps that a child learning to walk actually has to think about. After that, walking comes naturally.

Here are some of the strategies that you will find in this book:

Part One: *Social Strategies*. This first section is devoted to nonromantic relationships—making new friends, keeping old ones. Getting along with married couples. Meeting other singles who are doing things you like to do. Attending social occasions and planning them for your own guests and friends. Making connections through organizations, societies, activities, friends, and relatives.

Part Two: *Why No One Has to Be Lonely*. There's a difference between being alone and being lonely. Yes, you may be alone at many times, but that doesn't mean you have to be lonely, if you have command of some strategies for *dealing* with loneliness. Some people cope with loneliness by reshaping their attitudes toward being alone. For others, dealing with loneliness means building friendships, networking, developing a support system for times when they need it. Loneliness is not something to be feared. You *will* survive loneliness. And these are strategies that can help you master it.

Part Three: *Romantic Strategies*. If you are interested in developing a love relationship, what are the barriers? Are you looking in appropriate ways for an appropriate partner? Do you present an emotional obstacle course that others have to pass through in order to get to know you? Some singles are not looking for romantic relationships right now; others continue relationships without drawing any closer to marriage or living together with a romantic partner. What is right for you? And if it's a partner you want, what are some strategies for finding that person?

Part Four: *Getting Involved and Nurturing a Relationship*. What if you *know* your goal is involvement? How can you increase your chances of finding the person who is right for you? How do you nurture a relationship through the peaks and valleys of initial attraction and emotional attachment? And—if you are a parent—how can you manage the relationship while you are also giving the best care to your child or children? This section is a guide to helping you find a partner who shares your wish to have a lasting, strong relationship, if you decide that is your goal.

Part Five: *The Perils of Sex—What Do They Mean to You?* What risks are *you* willing to take—and what precautions will you use to safeguard your health? The Attitude Inventory found here is designed to help you make important choices about your sexual activities at this critical time.

Part Six: *Survival Strategies.* Housing, finances, taking care of yourself, and taking care of people who depend on you. Survival means looking after your own health and security needs, balancing work and play, and planning ahead for your own future.

The Community of Singles

There is strength in numbers.

What the media see as a phenomenon of our time— the number of men and women living on their own—is actually a strong, growing community with many shared understandings and values. That community began shaping itself in the sixties, seventies, and eighties. These have been the decades of enormous exploration in the areas of sexuality, alternative lifestyles, and sexual equality. The human-potential movement sprang to life during these decades. The divorce rate shot up. Both heterosexual and gay couples began living together openly. Men and women were more thoughtful about how many children they would have and when they would have them. Women became more likely to extend their professional training and experience, thus postponing their childbearing years.

All this was part of the sexual revolution. A large number of singles today are *products* of that revolution. Whether you were an adult or teenager when the sexual revolution began—or whether you were not even born yet—your life has certainly been affected in some way by the changes in lifestyles and sexual relationships that occurred during these decades.

But we are also living *after* the sexual revolution. The herpes scare of the late seventies and early eighties, followed by AIDS, has resulted in a swing of the pendulum. Now people are being much more careful about sex, and many who previously avoided monogamous relationships are seeking them out. Having experienced the sexual revolution, we are now experiencing a postrevolutionary phase, in which there is a gradual but significant readjustment of choices and priorities.

The result is that a new community has emerged that is unlike any that has come before. Millions of singles make up that community. We have many experiences in common. Many of us have similar expectations. Every day I meet single people who are pondering similar questions and looking for common solutions.

I've been a part of the singles community for many years. I was married at the ripe old age of twenty-two. My marriage ended a little over four years later.

At about the time of my divorce I was beginning the path toward a significant career change. Through a combination of hard work and being in the right place at the right time, I managed to own a successful accounting firm for a number of years beginning in my early twenties. I was doing quite well and it seemed like I had the perfect life. Yet somehow the thought of doing that kind of work for the rest of my life did not attract me. So, against a lot of advice, I began a long hard road toward a career change.

I sold my accounting firm and made an irrevocable commitment to the career of psychology—something that had always interested me as an avocation. I had to get two additional degrees. My marriage stopped work-ing as my lifestyle and professional interests changed. The year of my divorce, 1972, coincided with the time when I was going through this transition.

In the seventies, I began what were the first divorce groups for both men and women in the Philadelphia area. This was while I was pursuing my graduate work and in the early phases of my psychology career. When it came time to write a dissertation, I decided to study the problems of people who were experiencing separa-tion and divorce. This route not only got me through my doctoral studies, but also got me involved with the media, which has been a very integral part of my career for the past ten years.

Today I head a group clinical psychology practice in Philadelphia. I host psychology radio call-in programs both locally (for CBS, Philadelphia) and nationally (for NBC Talknet). I consult with several public and private organizations and am president of the Media Psychol-ogy Division of the American Psychological Associa-tion (APA). In my spare time I do a lot of work on the lecture circuit.

I have a seventeen-year-old daughter who does not live with me full time, but has always been as much a part of my life as though she did. I see her at least weekly, and we talk several times a week. She has always been with me every other weekend, and we're very close.

Throughout the years since my divorce, I've formed many meaningful relationships. Some have been sim-ply good friendships and others have been highly ro-mantic (two were live-in). Although I haven't remar-ried, I'm certainly not closed to the idea, but I would probably not consider marriage for its own sake. It would obviously have to be a logical next step with the right relationship.

What I have learned—and what I very happily practice myself—is what I teach my clients, and that is to be the architect of their own experiences, of their own lives. As far as we know, we have only one shot at life, and we have a duty to ourselves and our world to make it the best possible experience it can be.

I encourage you to be open to change and to be aware that the number of experiences life has to offer is infinite.

Many singles that I have met, both in my practice and elsewhere, live their lives *as though it were merely a dress rehearsal, and not the real show.* So your first step is to get out of that frame of mind. If I can help you to do that in any area of your life, then this book will have served the purpose for which it was written.

I encourage you to find what is right for you. After all, the advantage of being single is that you can shape your lifestyle, your work, your play, your time, your friendships, and your romances *for yourself.*

You can also make finding a relationship your goal, if that is what you want. But if that *is* what you want, then the goal is to choose relationships that are *right* for you. If you feel that you are moving in the direction of a relationship, then I would hope that you would choose an *appropriate* partner. That's what Part Three, *Romantic Strategies,* is all about.

What the Strategies in This Book Can Do for You

Throughout this book, you will find an emphasis on making choices. But before you can begin to make choices, you have to be convinced that you *can* make choices. You can separate the issues—decide what you want to do—and begin living toward your goals.

Not long ago, I worked with a client who had been married for five years. Kate was twenty-eight when she married. She had an MBA from Wharton (at the University of Pennsylvania) and was senior vice-president in the investment department of a Philadelphia bank. Her husband, Jay, also worked at the bank. Their schedules meshed perfectly, they spent a lot of time together as a couple, and Kate became very comfortable with their lifestyle. After they were married, they bought a house in the suburbs. Kate put many hours into decorating and furnishing their new home.

When Kate came to see me, she had just been through a long, messy divorce settlement. She and Jay had sold the house, and Kate had moved to a condominium. She was still in a lot of pain. Many emotional issues from the marriage were unsettled.

Up to the time she was married, Kate had enjoyed singles life. After her divorce, she expected to pick up again where she had left off five years before. Instead, she found that that was not possible. At least, not immediately. Too much had changed.

For one thing, she and Jay frequently had socialized with couples during the previous five years. Kate was friends with several married women. But after her divorce, she did not feel as comfortable being with a couple; she often felt like a fifth wheel. When she called her women friends, often they already had plans with their husbands. It was hard to see them on nights when they *weren't* doing things as a couple. And they did not invite her as frequently as they had when she was married.

Kate found the hours alone at home hard to fill. She thought too much about Jay. At times, she blamed herself. Who had really lost interest in their relationship first—he or she? Had her behavior or career aims *caused* the divorce?

Mealtimes were a problem. She felt lonely eating by herself at home, and she hated to go into a restaurant and sit down at a table by herself. After a hard day at work, she always had had someone to whom she could talk. Now there was no one at home to listen, no one to break her mood.

The condominium was nice, but it felt temporary. Kate had lost interest in decorating. She was certain that someone new would soon come into her life—so what was the point of making her home feel more permanent?

Kate began dating. She slept with only one of the men she dated—someone she had known since she was a teenager. She considered him more of a friend than a lover, but at least she felt comfortable about his sexual history. AIDS scared her; she was cautious.

In many respects, Kate *felt* like a teenager who was dating again. Yet she had very little interest in making a commitment to anybody at this time.

The Strategies

When Kate came in to counseling, the word she used most often was "loneliness." But that word represented many things to her. She was lonely because she found it difficult to make new friends. The hours that had flowed naturally now seemed hard to fill. The mundane details of her daily life bothered her, too—doing her laundry, balancing the checkbook, or watching TV by herself.

To Kate, none of these were separate issues. They all made up a single, large, unsolvable puzzle. Why couldn't she go back to the singles life she had enjoyed five years before? Why did everything seem so much more difficult *now* than it had *then?* Why did she feel so lonely? Was it just one thing—or a combination of everything?

As we started to work on these issues, Kate began to realize that she was out of practice at being single. Before she was married, she'd had her own set of strategies for socializing with friends, meeting men when she wanted to, dating, dining in or out, taking vacations, and planning weekends. When she was married to Jay, new patterns replaced those of the lifestyle she had built for herself.

Now that she was out of the relationship, the patterns of married life didn't hold up any more. Yet she clung to many of those patterns, reminding herself too often of her life with Jay. She often felt as if she should be moving toward living with somebody else. But there *was* nobody else—at least, not right now. So the familiar patterns only reminded her that someone was missing.

Kate needed a new set of strategies—

- Strategies for staying in touch with friends who were now married. How could she be a part of their lives and make them a part of hers? How persistent should she be? Would she have to let go of some of her married friends?
- Strategies for filling the hours alone. Kate had interests in sports, music, art, and many other activities. Some of these interests had been shunted aside during her married years. Now she needed to resurrect the activities that gave her pleasure and make them a larger part of her life. Where should she begin?
- Strategies for mealtimes. She said she wanted to make mealtimes less important to her. How could she feel better about eating alone? How could she plan

meals with other people? How could she overcome her resistance to dining alone in restaurants?

■ Strategies for networking. She wanted to start new friendships. But where should she begin? In a singles bar? A health club? A professional organization? Where was she most likely to meet the kind of people with whom she would feel comfortable, even if she wasn't looking for a relationship?

■ Strategies for getting over that temporary feeling. Somehow, she had to find a way to really move into her new home, feel comfortable there, and make it feel permanent. What was true of her home also held true for relationships. She wanted to remain open to relationships, but she needed strategies for enjoying single life without seeking it as a prelude to another relationship or to marriage.

■ Strategies for finding support. If a relationship wasn't right for her, who would support her emotionally when she was down and needed help?

We did not try to begin these strategies all at once. They were introduced in small increments, assigned as specific, weekly tasks. But the results that Kate saw in herself reinforced the value of *having* strategies and *acting* on them.

As the weeks passed and she completed her assignments, Kate underwent a change of attitude. She was steadily getting more adept at living the good singles life. Her emotions changed, and as they did, instead of loneliness, she felt more positive about herself. She had begun to master *the art of living single*.

Single life had threatened her. It had been intimidating. She had protected herself from that intimidation by thinking of it as something transitory. But thinking of herself as being in transition had only made her feel lonelier.

Finally, Kate reached a stage where she could say, "Being single *might* be temporary. On the other hand, if I'm always single, I can still be comfortable and fulfilled, and enjoy my life."

I hope this book will help you to master the strategies of living single so you can reach that position, as Kate did, where you can say, "I have designed a good single life for myself." In fact, I recommend that you begin a personal notebook that you can write in as you are reading this book—and refer to later. This notebook will help you respond to the Attitude Inventories in this book, and it can also be a personal journal where you write observations and advice for yourself.

Living Single was written with the express purpose of being *useful* to you. Find the strategies that are right for you—borrow them, adapt them, use them—then shape a design that fits who you are and what you need.

Being free to design your own life is an exciting adventure.

Good luck!

MICHAEL S. BRODER
PHILADELPHIA, PA

Part One

Social Strategies

When you're single, only one person is responsible for your social schedule—and that's *you!*

That can be both good and bad. The good part, of course, is that you don't have to check in with anyone before you decide to go somewhere, meet someone, or do something on the spur of the moment.

When I ask singles specifically what they like about being single, their answers play a recurring theme: "I like the freedom. I can do whatever I want to do, without asking anyone else."

Doreen, a thirty-five-year-old college professor who was divorced six years ago, made a comparison between being single and being married. "I think the highs are higher, the lows are lower—but there's more drama, less predictability. And I really like the highs— meeting someone new, being able to take off and do something. There are a lot of unknowns. You never know what's going to happen tomorrow."

So that's the good part. But there's a catch here. *You are only as good at socializing as you make yourself.*

Look in the mirror. There is your social director. You decide when you are going to eat out and when you will go to a movie this week. You are looking at the person who is responsible for setting up your activities on Saturday night, Sunday morning, next week, next month, and next holiday.

The person in the mirror also has to handle the socializing that occurs every day. Is that person— *you!*—going to start up a conversation with someone new at the office. At the next party, is your social director—*you!*— going to meet three new people, and arrange for you to have lunch with one of them?

Thinking of yourself as your own social director can actually be the move that gets you out of your shell.

Self-Talk Strategies

There is only one drawback to being your own social director. If you are a little weak in one area, you don't necessarily have a partner who can compensate. On the other hand, you don't have to *compromise* with a partner either. It often has been noted of couples that when one person wants to do something and the other person doesn't, the person who *doesn't* usually wins.

Be aware of your own shortcomings as social director. Make up for them where necessary. For instance:

■ Are you good at making long-range plans? If not, you may end up inviting people at the last minute. Some friends can adapt to that, but others might not be able to. So you *could* be limiting your range of possibilities by being a spur-of-the-moment planner.

■ Do you wait for people to call? No social director would let you get away with that. As your own director, you have to be someone who calls other people, makes plans, and sets things up.

■ Do you reciprocate? Remember, you are responsible for the whole works—the invitations, the follow-up calls, the thank-yous, the little meaningful signals that you enjoyed being invited somewhere and that you want to reciprocate. Yes, you are a social secretary as well as a social director.

■ Do you pursue your goals? You may have to pursue your purpose with dogged determination. Whether you are getting the right group together for a party or just making sure that you meet up with someone you *want* to meet, it's up to you to make it happen.

Never Mind Romance

When you concentrate on socializing activities, you are not necessarily looking for romantic involvement. The strategies in this section will focus on *non*romantic relationships. Lightning can strike any time, of course. But you will not be an effective social director if your only goal is to make a match for yourself or even for others. That's mixing tasks.

Instead, ask yourself, "Now, with whom would I like to be *friends?*" "What activities would I enjoy *whether or not* I encounter a romantic partner?" "How can I have a pleasant, rewarding experience with (or without) some kind of companionship this weekend?"

In this entire section, we're focusing on things that *you* like doing for yourself, keeping you content and comfortable in an area that you may have found to be most difficult. If you can do that, you're ahead of the game. And don't worry—we'll get to the romance issues. But for now, remember, you can't let the expectation of romance determine all your social strategies. That's just not being fair to *you*.

Some Ways to Go

If you have now accepted the position of social director, your main responsibility is to interview yourself and find out what you want from your social life. Your priorities might change at any time. But it's important to figure out what those priorities are.

What will you enjoy? What do you *love* doing? Picture your ideal entertainment. Picture the people you want to be with. Picture a setting that seems attractive. Then let's look at some strategies for getting you there.

Below is a Social Strategizing Self-Inventory (SSSI) that gives you an opportunity to look at your priorities. Look at the fourteen goals on this list, and either check off the most important ones, or number them in order of importance. This is a chance to evaluate which strategies you most need to work on. Use a notebook to copy out and fill in the inventory that follows.

SOCIAL STRATEGIZING SELF-INVENTORY (SSSI)

Check off the items that are of concern in your life now. (You may want to rank them in order of importance and go to the sections of this book that most address your particular needs.)

1. _____ I want to invite out other people more often, and I want others to invite *me* out more often.

2. _____ I need to have more sports and fitness activities in my life.

3. _____ I want to spend more time with other singles.

4. ____ I want to entertain in my own home.

5. ____ I want to "get away from it all" and still have fun even if I'm by myself.

6. ____ I want to get to know people at work.

7. ____ I would like to relate to people in a more intellectual or spiritual atmosphere.

8. ____ I want to get more involved in a hobby or avocation.

9. ____ I would like to have more fun and feel lighter around other people.

10. ____ I want to get closer to my friends who are in couples.

11. ____ I would like to reestablish contacts and ties with former friends.

12. ____ I would like to become involved in more social, political, or community activities.

13. ____ I want to get more enjoyment out of my vacations.

14. ____ I want more ideas for enjoying my weekends and holidays.

Using Your SSSI

What are your priorities? What does your social life *need*—and what are you getting now?

The following chapters outline some strategies that could work for you.

In your notebook, underline, take notes, or put exclamation points in the margin. Even if the strategy doesn't sound like something you would do, at least consider it before ruling it out. This is an opportunity to stretch some of your boundaries and to try things you may never have done before.

By taking action, your reward can be a new set of social strategies that can benefit you for a lifetime.

Chapter 1

How Do I Get Invited Out More Often?

Recently, I was at a party with a large group of people including couples and singles. Connie, a friend of mine who is a lawyer, was also there. I noticed during the evening that she talked to several men and women she was meeting for the first time. Toward the end of the party, I overheard her making plans to meet with one of the women the following week.

I was impressed at how quickly she had struck up an acquaintance that seemed headed for friendship. When I was talking with her later, I asked her why this kind of socializing seemed to go so easily for her.

"I'm open with people, and I'm curious about other people," she said. "So that must get them interested. I'm always open to disclosing things about myself."

She does not hesitate to make plans on the spot:

A lot of people I meet are single, and I'm single. I don't like to be home alone. So it's easy for me to say, "I'd like to talk to you some more. Let's go out for a drink some time." Or if I have a common

21

interest with that person, we'll make plans around something we'd both like to do.

I asked her whether people were ever unreceptive to a spontaneous invitation like that.

Very rarely unreceptive. If they are, I'll drop it and it's no big deal. But more likely, they'll say, "Let's do that," and then not follow through. So I'll try to make a date right there—or get a phone number so I can follow through by giving a call the next day to make plans. I've made many friends this way—and people approach me. So I don't feel as if I'm pushing. I'd just like to see them again, and I want to make that happen.

What impressed me about Connie's approach was summed up in that key word—*openness*. With anyone she met for the first time, she was *open* to the possibility of friendship. She gave each person a chance. She revealed something of herself, and she showed curiosity about the other person. If there was an equal and open exchange of views, she assumed that the other person would like to see her again as much as she would like to see the other person.

The Assertive Approach

Connie's approach may sound very assertive, and it is. And her socializing strategy has been a powerful tool for her in making friends and making her feel secure and comfortable with her life as a single.

Your own approach will depend on your personal style. If you have some difficulty getting invited out— or inviting others out—here are some points to keep in mind:

BE DIRECT

It's okay to announce what you like to do. In fact, it's essential if the other person is going to get to know you. There's nothing wrong with saying:

"I love to go to the theater. Any time I have the chance, I'll go!"

"I used to play a lot of Scrabble. It was fun. I'd like to start doing that again."

"I'd love to try that new Vietnamese restaurant."

You *plant a seed*. Is the other person interested? Does your comment lead to talk about theater, Scrabble words, or new restaurants? Why not make plans on the spot to get together again?

IF YOU WANT TO BE INCLUDED, SAY SO

It never hurts to ask. Andrea, a twenty-seven-year-old paralegal, told me:

I always used to get a twinge when someone else was doing something I really wanted to do. I would try to think of subtle ways to get invited, and if the other person didn't invite me, I would think they really didn't want me to go.

I learned my lesson. A friend of mine was going to a figure skating championship. When I heard about it, I really wanted to go. But I didn't say anything. Afterward, I happened to mention my interest in the event. My friend said, "Good Lord, you should have *told* me. We had an extra ticket and we ended up giving it away."

That taught me. I don't hedge any more. If there's something I'd really like to do, I just say,

"That sounds great. I'd love to go. Can I come along?" Of course, I use common sense. I won't intrude on a weekend-for-two that someone has planned. But there are a lot of things where people are glad to have company. I'm not going to miss out just because I'm afraid to speak up.

This openness about what she wants to do definitely has worked for Andrea. She is very active and she is doing things she *likes* to do with other people.

BE OPEN TO SUGGESTION

You can let the other person suggest something. Some people think they'll look helpless or vulnerable if they say, "I'm free this . . . [weekend/evening/Thursday night], and I'd like to get together with you. Can you suggest anything?"

When I mentioned this approach to Kenny, who works in public relations, he said, "I don't like to do that. I'd rather have a plan. If I can't think of something definite to do with that person, I'm not going to suggest getting together."

I pointed out that he might be missing the opportunity of knowing someone better. He was also putting a lot of pressure on himself. Why should it be *his* responsibility to choose the time, the place, and the occasion?

Kenny agreed that he would try the strategy. At the next social occasion, he was talking to a man who belonged to the American Society of Journalists and Authors. Kenny got himself invited to the next lecture. It was something that he had really wanted to do, but he never would have thought of it himself.

Why assume that the best-laid plans are the ones that you make? Other people have things going on that might interest you. See if you can get yourself included. New experiences are just around the corner.

SHOW YOUR INTEREST

Ask for an invitation. Have you just heard about a party, an event, or an occasion that you would like to attend? If you want to go, why not find out if you can get an invitation?

Again, you can be assertive without being pushy or too aggressive. There is usually a polite way to say: "That sounds like something I'd really enjoy."

That approach might not get you an automatic invitation, of course. But it signals the other person that you're interested, you'd like to attend, and you think you'd enjoy yourself. Even if that person can't get an invitation for you this time, he or she might think of you next time. Either way, you haven't lost anything.

What Style Is Right for You?

As you think about your own strategies, ask yourself what feels comfortable. Do you have a hard time being direct? Are you afraid the other person will rudely say "No" or otherwise reject your request?

If rejection is a major concern, ask yourself: "What's the *worst* thing that can happen?"

At worst, the other person might become evasive or think of an excuse why you can't get together. Some amount of rejection is inevitable. Even though it's momentarily unpleasant, fearing it will only make you avoid the reaching out you want to do.

But you have everything to gain if your strategy works. You could make a new friend. You could be invited to places where you would like to go and have new experiences. A whole new social group might open up for you.

The down-side risk is small. And the up-side possibilities are tremendous.

But what about being *too* pushy? Do you think that might be a problem for you?

If so, there is a simple attitude survey. Ask yourself, "Would I be offended if someone said to *me*, '_____'?" Then answer yes or no.

In your notebook, ask yourself the following:

ATTITUDE SURVEY

Would I be offended if someone said to me . . .

"I'd like to get together for coffee sometime soon. When can we meet?"   YES____ NO____

"Can I give you a call at the office tomorrow so we can make plans?"   YES____ NO____

"Could you let me know next time you're going to the game? I'd like to go along."   YES____ NO____

"I'm signing up for a film festival. Would you like me to send the schedule?"   YES____ NO____

"I don't have a thing planned for Sunday morning—do you want to have brunch?"
                                                                   YES____ NO____

"It's been good talking with you, and I'd like us to get together again. What's good for you?"
                                                                   YES____ NO____

"Next weekend is completely open for me. Would you like to plan something?"   YES____ NO____

If you try the survey above, I think you'll find that, in most cases, you wouldn't be offended at all. In fact, if you're enjoying a conversation with that person, you probably would be pleased to be asked.

The good news is, most people that you *do* question will share your view. So why not ask?

Chapter 2

How Sports and Fitness Activities Can Open Up Your Life

Fortunately, these are boom times for sports and physical fitness. There are many ways to turn sports activities into opportunities for socializing.

Attitude is important. If you participate in a sport *primarily* to meet someone of the opposite sex, you may be disappointed. Make this an activity that first and foremost you'll enjoy *for yourself*.

Here are just a few of the alternatives:

■ *Health clubs.* Many singles belong. One client who does aerobics three times a week told me, "Aerobics is *my* time. I'm with people, but I'm doing it for myself. I come out feeling really good."

Since she joined the class, however, she has made several new friends.

A male friend plays racquetball in a competitive round robin every Tuesday night. He joined with another male friend. They usually have a couple of drinks afterward. Other members of the club have started to join them, and now there is an informal group that gets together after every round robin.

■ *Organized leagues*. Almost every sport in the nation has organized amateur leagues. You can get more information from your local recreation facility, from a sports organization, or by talking to other people who are interested in your sport.

In New York, publishing companies, advertising agencies, and law firms have their own softball leagues. There's also a Broadway Show League, featuring actors and actresses who have appeared in Broadway shows. No matter where you are, if softball is a game you enjoy, you're likely to find local teams for every level of player.

For other sports, there are national, regional, and local organizations. If you join a tennis, golf, racquetball, skiing, sailing, running, rowing, bowling, or squash club, you get a double benefit. You are surrounded by people who enjoy the same sport you do— which tends to raise your level of involvement and interest. And as a side benefit, you have the chance to get involved in club-related activities like fund-raising and planning social events.

■ *Coaching kids*. Along with sports activities that you do for yourself, you might want to consider coaching or umpiring neighborhood or city league teams. You can make contacts through the school athletic department, or talk to parents whose children are involved in sports. Organizations are always looking for adults to help out. You'll meet parents (some single), get to help some kids, and pass along some skills that you picked up in your days as a basketball, field hockey, soccer, football, or baseball star.

Chapter 3

Enriching Your Life with Other Singles

If you have avoided some singles activities because you labeled them "meat markets," you might want to consider going with your own agenda. You can take along your own group. You can go to flirt, if that's what you want. Or you can enjoy one evening's worth of superficial relationships. You can make friends (see Chapter 1 for strategies). Or you can go to a singles activity just for the atmosphere.

In other words, when *you have your own agenda*, you can always enjoy socializing whether or not you meet anyone special.

Where to Find Singles Activities

Almost every community of any size has activities for singles. In a metropolitan area, of course, your selection is much wider.

Whether you live in a small town or large city, you're likely to find singles activities at churches and synagogues. You don't need to have any kind of strong religious affiliation or convictions. Activities often are organized around nonreligious events.

YMCAs, YWCAs, and YMHAs usually have programs for singles. You are also likely to meet singles through professional organizations. Or consider a writers' group, a repertory theater company, an artists' co-op—any kind of organization that attracts single people who are doing things that interest you.

Here are some other ways to find single-scene activities in your area:

- Check local newspapers and magazines. In larger cities, you'll find guidebooks that list organizations catering to singles. *How to Find a Date: A Complete Directory for Singles* by Carolyn Mordecai (Crown, 1986) has listings of organizations that help singles find other singles all around the country. Although it is really a book about dating, there is no reason why you can't join one of the clubs, organizations, or networks listed in the book just to *meet* people.

Again, it's a matter of having *your own agenda!*

- Try some singles bars or nightclubs. Go alone or with companions.

"I *like* singles bars," a friend told me, "but not necessarily to meet people to *date*. You're walking into a room full of people who want to meet people. How many places can you go to do that?"

- Do things you've never done before. There are many activities for singles where you can indulge your interests, develop new tastes, or just be certain of new experiences. Typical is a group in Philadelphia called Theatre for Singles, that, once a month, travels to New York for a theater, ballet, or opera performance.

Dinners for Singles is a group sponsored by the Learning Annex. The group meets at a restaurant, and everyone changes seats between courses, so you continue to meet new people throughout the meal.

To find out about similar groups in your area, check the listings in your local newspapers. Sunday's and Friday's papers are especially likely to have sections that list singles events.

Once you have a topic or focus in mind, you can get leads by going directly to a resource. For instance, if you are looking for a theater group for singles, try calling a theater. If you're looking for something that has to do with travel, try contacting a travel agency.

The larger the city, the easier it will be to find local resources. But wherever you are, you are likely to find clubs and organizations that are meant for people of wide-ranging interests. There are gourmet clubs for singles; supermarkets for singles; lectures and discussions; great-books clubs; clubs for lunch dates; clubs for geniuses, for widowed people, for symphony lovers, for bridge players, for chess players. Ask. Find out what's happening in your area. Remember, whatever you join, it's not a lifetime membership. The commitment is just for as long as you enjoy it, as long as you meet people, or as long as it fits your personal agenda for socializing.

Chapter 4

Entertaining Successfully at Home

If you want to entertain on a large scale, you might want to try a big party.

The big party is a grand occasion that takes place on your turf and on your own terms. It may involve extensive preparations. It may stretch your resources. But the event is usually worth the effort and planning that go into it. There are several ways to plan a big party:

- *Around an occasion*. A significant birthday (yours!). May Day. Halloween. A summer solstice party. The anniversary of the completion of the Eiffel Tower. Mother's Day. Supernova Day. Publication Day. An opening. A closing. A promotion. Any occasion is worthy of a sumptuous big party.
- *Around a person*. If you are in a business where celebrities, CEOs, or prominent personalities appear on the scene, consider holding the next reception at your place if this is realistic.
- *Around a theme*. One of Philadelphia's literary figures who has deplored the passing of the Age of

Elegance organizes an occasional party around a theme of his choice. One year it was Cole Porter music and black-and-white Art Deco. Another year it was opera, northern Italian cuisine, and a strolling violinist.

For this event, you might want to solicit the help of one or two friends who can assist you. If you're on a tight budget, plan the main courses with your friends, have selected people contribute hors d'oeuvres and everyone else bring wine, beer, or soft drinks.

If you can afford it—or save for it—you may also want to consider a catered event, especially if it is a sit-down meal. For a large crowd, you will need an open bar.

If your place is too small for such an event, investigate locations you can rent. Again, whether you can afford it will depend on your budget. But you may be surprised at some of the elegant rooms that can be rented out for a relatively small fee.

One way to find out about such places is by asking a caterer or checking with hotels. You might also look up various clubs or organizations in your area, or ask people who frequently hold parties or business functions. Florists, bakeries, and liquor stores that cater for parties might also know about locations for rent.

This is a great opportunity to indulge your fantasies and be as lavish as you choose. Display your prowess as a broker of "social power."

Once-a-Month Events

If you know a group of people who like to do things together, why not set up a regular schedule? Once a month is usually often enough. If you have a number of people in the group, agree to hold the event in someone else's house each month. Consider:

■ Once-a-month backgammon, or bridge, or dinner, or Boggle, or poker, or quilting, or video movies—or even no theme, just relaxing conversation. If you make it a monthly event, and rotate apartments or homes, you'll get used to the idea that once a month you'll see the same group of people.

Kathy, who grew up on the Main Line, told me:

> I used to turn up my nose at my mother's Thursday-night bridge club. Hey, I'm an urbanite. I don't do that. Then I realized that our women's network group had almost turned into the same thing. After I lost interest in that group, I decided to start something completely different. We get together once a month at about eight o'clock and serve hors d'oeuvres and wine and have a talk fest. We call it Wednesday Night Winos. We have twelve women in the group, and we rotate. That way, each of us hosts it just once a year. I still get to see all those women I've kept in touch with. It's fun.

Before-or-After Events

For minimum preparation and maximum comfort, consider having people over before or after a show or a game. This can be more advantageous than an extended party. If you have people over beforehand, everyone comes more or less on time, because they know they only have an hour or two before they have to leave again. You don't have to provide a major meal, either.

If it's afterward, you might have drinks, dessert, and coffee. But be sure to let people know that's *all* you're serving, so they will have a light supper before the show or game.

No Place Like Home

If you find that you avoid having people over to your house or apartment, you might ask yourself why. It could be that you just prefer meeting someone outside to avoid a lot of preparation. And if so, that's fine. But if it's because you don't like the way your home looks, you might consider some strategies for improving your home environment. If possible, make it suitable for entertaining so you feel comfortable doing it.

- Get out some magazines. Start dreaming a little. If you like to hunt used-furniture stores, you can find some wonderful pieces buried under layers of paint. Refinishing takes patience, but it's rewarding when the new piece is finally done.

Redecorating, renovating, and dressing up your place can be expensive, but if you are willing to do the work yourself and be patient with your progress, do the work in sections—sealing off one room or one area at a time—so you can keep the project going without disrupting your whole life. If you know someone who has a similar type of project, arrange a trade-off: you'll help them for a while, if they'll help you. Renovation is much more bearable if someone else is working alongside you.

But it can be fun, too. And the end result is worth it. Having a place where you can bring people warms it up for *you*. I've never known anyone to regret the energy they put into making their home a pleasant place in which to entertain.

- Do you dislike cooking? If so, perhaps you can get your friends involved. Or you might find good takeout food or someone who can cater or help you clean up for a reasonable price.

Recently, a friend told me, "I just stopped having dinners. What's the point? I never get to see anyone at my own party. I spend all day cooking, all night serving, and all morning cleaning up."

I gave her the name of a college service that sends out students to serve and clean up. For about sixty dollars for the evening, her next dinner became a stellar event.

Chapter 5

Getting Away from It All on Your Own

In a group I was conducting for newly divorced singles, a woman I will call Lonnie told us about the weekend of her big escape:

> I was completely fed up. Kent [her ex] was on my mind all the time. Things were going horribly at work. I couldn't think of anything to do. I picked up a book on country inns and read about a beautiful restored farmhouse in Vermont. I didn't know anything about it, but the description sounded nice. I called and talked to the woman who ran the place with her husband. She said the place had a huge porch with rocking chairs and it overlooked a big lake. When she said they would serve me breakfast in bed, I was sold.
>
> That weekend was the best thing I could have done. The owners were wonderful. They introduced me to the other guests, and after dinner we sat around the fire, sipped brandy, and talked about the state of the world. I completely forgot myself. It was perfect. I'm going again next year.

The Great Escape

As others in the group shared their experiences with getting-away-from-it-all, we began to see that these were usually more than one-time events. People discovered new places. They found things they liked to do. What seemed like "escapes" were in fact leading them into interesting new experiences.

There was a lot of variety among the great escapes that people mentioned:

- *Weekends in the city.* Many hotels offer special weekend rates for off-season times of the year. Some people in the group took advantage of these offers to get into town for a show, sightseeing, shopping, or the opening of an art exhibition.
- *Relaxation.* Lonnie's great weekend in Vermont was not unique. Other people had their favorite places at the shore or cozy ski lodges where they went every winter. They mentioned two- and three-day getaways to places as diverse as Williamsburg, Atlantic City, and Disney World. One man who had a very flexible schedule said he was on a special list for quick trips to the Bahamas and Virgin Islands. Whenever a charter passenger cancelled and a space opened up on a flight, the seat was his at a bargain-basement rate.
- *Socializing getaways.* A summer rental shared among friends can be a perfect summer retreat. Several people in the group who were just getting over relationships said the summer rental taught them to enjoy being single again. You can meet a whole new group of friends this way. One woman said she had shared a house with friends at the shore for a number of years. "My summers wouldn't be complete without it. It's an escape—but I'm surrounded by familiar faces, and I can socialize if I want to."

■ *Meeting friends at an out-of-town event.* Some of the baseball and football aficionados considered their attendance at games mandatory. Whether a game was home or away, they made plans to meet friends. They planned an entire season of weekends around a football or baseball schedule.

Among the non-sports-fans there were some other ideas. One woman goes to the Shakespeare Festival in Ontario every year. She sends her schedule to a couple of friends, and they make arrangements to attend the same performances.

An avid equestrian schedules her getaways around Grand Prix jumping events on the East Coast.

One man who's a sports-car driver goes to several rallies a year. Invariably, he meets up with the same people he's seen the year before. They catch up, talk about cars, have a great weekend, and then say good-bye . . . for another year.

Business, academic, and professional conferences are excellent places to meet people. If you do not go every year, you may find that your social skills are tested the first time you attend. It may seem as if everyone knows each other from years past, and you're the outsider. But remember, you have something in common with everyone there, and there are always parties and meetings that you can attend.

At conferences, mealtimes are a great time to mix with other people. Usually you will see people whom you meet in various sessions—and they are usually open to letting you join them. People quite freely exchange business cards, and fellow professionals can be contacted later on. Even if you do not easily approach people under ordinary circumstances, the knowledge that other people are members of your field somehow makes them more accessible. (The fact that they're often wearing name tags helps with introductions, too.)

You can also use a conference strategically if you want to make a geographical move. Sandy, a reading specialist, was recently divorced. She wanted to fulfill a dream of moving to the West Coast, and she used conferences to help her achieve her goal. She attended a number of West Coast conferences and at each one she made contacts and gathered names and addresses. By the time she was ready to move, she had already established a network of people in her field.

So if you go with the attitude that you want to meet as many people as possible, you can find people who share many of your professional and personal interests. And they will introduce you to others! The network spreads quickly at these occasions.

Chapter 6

How Do I Get to Know People Better at Work?

"I'm tired of seeing the same faces every day," complained a young man who called in to my radio program. "I work long hours. The only people I see are people in the office. It's always the same routine and, frankly, I'm bored with them."

As I asked him a few questions, it quickly became apparent that the "same old faces" were really just that—faces. The young man knew many people in the office well enough to say hello to and talk with about office matters. But beyond that, their lives were a blank to him. I pointed out that his life was probably a mystery to them, as well.

Often, getting to know people at work means escalating the relationship. The goal is to break through the same-old-faces routine. If you've been in the same job for a long time, it may take a new jolt to get your relationships with people to a new level.

How can you start socializing with people you see every day? Here are some ways to try:

■ Be the person who starts conversations—in the elevator, around the coffee machine, or over the desk. Get into new territory—children, vacations, books, movies, sports, clothes. Show some curiosity about the other person's whole life, not just routine work matters. Be more open about what's happening with you.

■ Be the person who takes other people out for special occasions. The office-wide birthday is fine as a celebration, but it may not do anything to extend *your* relationship with that person. Why not take the birthday person out to lunch, apart from the crowd?

■ Celebrate the other person's promotion with a lunch or with drinks after work. You might be surprised what a positive reaction you get from that person. These are times when a person feels special, and they will enjoy your company as well as the recognition you're giving them.

Somewhat later in my call-in program, a woman named Marilyn recalled inviting the head of her department out for a drink:

> To other people in my department, it seemed very daring. But it didn't seem so at the time. The director of my department had just won an award. We were talking about it, and I said, "Well, why don't we celebrate?" When I invited her for a drink, she was very pleased. The award meant a lot to her, but because no one in the department said anything, she was feeling disappointed. She opened up. We got to know each other a lot better, and we can talk about things outside the office. Just knowing her that much better has *totally* changed the feel of the office for me.

Be a person who shows up at company gatherings. "I used to skip the picnics," the creative director of an ad agency told me. "I figured they were just employee-relations exercises. Then I realized I was missing out. Friendships, relationships, and politics were all going down at those picnics. I *was* missing out. Call it corporate culture or office politics—if you're outside it, you miss a lot."

If your company has a softball team, a volleyball team, or a volunteer group that is open to everyone in the company . . . join! When you are with those people in a different environment, you may find many of the social opportunities you want are right in your workplace. You will discover many opportunities to develop friendships.

Chapter 7

Relating to People in a More Intellectual or Spiritual Atmosphere

In one of my therapy groups, we got into a discussion around some issues that were troubling one member of the group. In his own words:

> When I look back at the way I was in college, I wonder why I've changed so much. I used to have some intellectual excitement that I could share with people. I remember staying up until all hours of the morning in my freshman dorm talking about social issues, existential issues, the meaning of life, all that kind of thing. At work, it's all numbers and management problems. I feel as if my brain is drying up.

Some other members of the group pointed out that the group itself gave him the opportunity to talk about issues that were important to him. But he believed that his interests went beyond the group's. He wanted to deal with a number of social and religious issues—questions of belief, responsibility, social commitment, and meaningful action. So we discussed some places and ways he might find that kind of stimulation. Among the suggestions:

- Educational institutions. No one who has the desire to learn needs to stay out of the classroom. Colleges have adult courses in every subject area. Adult learning centers often have good introductions to new fields that you might want to explore.

- Discussion groups. Outside conventional educational institutions, there are groups that meet to discuss novels, plays, and great issues. If you like writing, or enjoy the challenge, you might join a night-school class or creative writing seminar. Many issues come to the fore when people begin trying to express their thoughts and experiences in writing.

- Assertiveness training, motivational seminars and classes, and self-help groups. Joining one of these is a good way to meet people who are in some kind of transition or process of change.

- Other groups focus on meditation, spiritual growth, astrology, and New Age concepts. If you join a group that's compatible with your own concerns and relates to your spiritual growth, the experience can be very rewarding. You always have the option of withdrawing from the group if your thinking begins to change or if the atmosphere becomes coercive rather than stimulating.

- Religious groups. I've had many clients say to me, especially in their middle to late thirties, "You know, my faith has started to be important to me again." Adults in transition often look back to religious roots that were planted in childhood. As those become more important again, they may begin looking for some kind of spiritual connection. You may begin going to services in the faith you were taught as a child—or this may be a time to look into other religions as well.

- Singles groups run by a therapist or counselor.
I've been involved in many of these groups myself, and
I've seen them produce very big rewards for individuals dealing with issues of separation, divorce, and living single.

Chapter 8

Getting Involved in Hobbies and Avocations

Dan began playing the guitar when he was eight. He took lessons, helped start a band when he was thirteen, and continued playing through high school. By the time he was seventeen, the band was getting so many gigs that Dan thought about skipping college and leading a musician's life. But he was a good student, and at his parents' urging he finally chose the college route.

While in college, Dan occasionally filled in for the guitar player in a campus band. But when he made the choice to go into premed, he no longer had time to practice. By the time he entered medical school, the guitar was gathering dust in the attic.

When Dan became my client, he was forty-two years old. He had not talked about his band in a long time. But when he did, his face lit up. Those days obviously held some good memories for him. I asked why he didn't play any more.

"I haven't practiced for twenty years," he said. "You know what I'd sound like?"

I suggested he forget his concerns and try again. A few weeks later he told me he had started to play again, and he was enjoying it. He hadn't completely lost the touch after all. After a few months, he got together with a group of friends for a jam session, and they liked the sound.

Now he and his friends do an occasional nightclub gig, though he has no interest in getting into the music business. His reward comes from playing the guitar again, getting together with friends, and occasionally entertaining an audience.

Now Is the Time

Singles life gives us an extraordinary opportunity to pursue avocations that can be tremendously rewarding. If you have gone through college or graduate school, devoted yourself to a career, been involved in relationships or marriage, you know what the time crunch does to extracurricular activities. When study, work, and relationships make demands on you, the small-scale, leisure-time activities are the first to be discarded.

Right now may be the time to *bring them back.* What were the things that *used* to hold your attention, give you pleasure? What did you enjoy doing by yourself or with your friends before responsibilities, obligations, and career took over your life?

Here are some avocations that some very contented singles have mentioned:

- Stamp collecting
- Model making
- Painting
- Sewing
- Weaving
- Dancing (ballroom, jazz, country, ethnic, ballet, modern)

- Knitting
- Model railroading
- Vocal and instrumental music
- Throwing pottery
- Reading
- Bird-watching
- Operating ham radio
- Butterfly collecting
- Crochet, embroidery, quiltmaking
- Meteorology
- Basketmaking, macramé
- Gardening
- Writing
- Metalworking
- Home electronics
- Boatbuilding and model boatbuilding
- Personal growth
- Kite making
- Carving
- Doll making
- Record collecting
- Calligraphy
- Juggling
- Cooking
- Film, video, and photography
- Playing chess
- Scuba diving
- Wine tasting

What Do You Love Doing?

In your notebook, list three hobbies or activities that you really enjoyed doing in the past.

What preparations do you need to make if you want to begin pursuing one or more of those activities again? When could you start? What do you need to get going again? New equipment? A place to work? Do you need lessons? Do you want to talk to some other people who are involved? Should you join an organization? Are there books or magazines that could guide you in getting started?

Now try some imaging. What will it mean to you to get involved in an avocation that you really enjoy? Can you derive enjoyment just from the *doing*—or do you need to see constant improvement or some end product? Is the competition what turns you on? What will the rewards be?

Avocations add richness to life. The more you pursue what you really like doing, the more it becomes yours. It's not an obligation. It's not *work*. It's something you really want to do that counts. Perhaps something you love. When you return to an avocation that you truly love, you are making a very *positive* affirmation about the way you want to enjoy your life.

What Could You Love Doing?

In addition to avocations you have pursued in the past, you can begin today to pursue a new hobby or line of interest. If your goals are realistic, age usually doesn't matter. True, you aren't likely to become a concert violinist if you start playing violin at the age of forty-five. But you *can* learn to play at any age.

When you are learning something new, you also begin to interact with people in new, perhaps exciting ways. Consider:

■ You learn quickly. Many teachers are delighted to have an adult pupil who is motivated and interested. If you want to go at a faster pace, any teacher is likely to support that effort.

■ You ask questions. Whether you're just getting started as a lepidopterist, lapidarian, or bibliophile, you will find experts who are enthusiastic, knowledgeable, and willing to share.

■ You ask for help. When you begin searching for resources, you will find many people who can help you. Many of them *like* to be asked.

Richer Rewards

About a year ago, a friend of mine began writing short stories and submitting them to literary magazines. Glenda is thirty-seven years old and in the insurance business. She had never done any creative writing before.

Glenda asked me whether I knew any fiction writers in Philadelphia or New York. I didn't, but I recommended that she attend some readings and try to meet people.

During Glenda's next business trip to New York, she went to a reading sponsored by the *Paris Review*. She met a published short-story writer and asked if he would critique her work. A couple of weeks later, she got a long letter from him praising her work. He suggested a West Coast magazine that might be interested in her writing. The writer knew the editor, and told Glenda that he would mention her.

Knowing she would probably see a lot of rejection slips, Glenda set up a schedule for sending out her stories. She set some realistic writing goals—four or five pages a week—and put aside Saturday and Sunday mornings for her writing time.

Her story was accepted by the West Coast magazine.

Having that story accepted has given her a great boost. It is the first step in realizing a dream. She has discovered that she loves to write, and she likes talking to people about her own writing and theirs. She has joined the Philadelphia Writers Group, and she is making more contacts in New York.

If she were setting out to become a big commercial writer, these little steps over a protracted period of time would be frustrating. But she is going for more intrinsic rewards. And finding them.

Chapter 9

How to Initiate Good Times in Your Life

Kristin, a thirty-five-year-old teacher, says she is often the one who gets other people to do things:

> I find myself being the coordinator. I'm the initiator—the one who makes the phone calls to get my group of friends together.
>
> But that's the type of person I am. I like to be out and on the go. I think some of my single friends tend to get lazy. Or they go into their own little world. They sit back and wait.
>
> With these friends I have taken on the role of the person who's always saying, "Would you like to do this? Would you like to go *here* or *there?*" When they do go along with me, they have fun. But sometimes it's hard to get them going.

Listen to Your Social Director

It may seem obvious, but one way to have fun is to go places where people *do* have fun. Maybe you'll want someone else to go with you, and that could mean a few phone calls. Put yourself in the place of the person getting your call. How would you like it if someone asked you to . . .

- Go to the amusement park and ride a roller coaster
- Take a balloon ride this weekend
- See the Big Apple Circus when it's in town
- Play poker
- Go to Walt Disney World
- Take a bus to the nearest resort
- Go hang gliding
- Pack a picnic lunch and go to the duck pond
- Toss a Frisbee

You may have to be the one who does the inviting. As Kristin noted, people don't do these things spontaneously. Often they have to be called and nudged.

When your social director tells you it's time to have fun, heed the inner voice. It's usually telling you something important. Now is the time for light entertainment, fresh air, fun with people, and goofing off.

Hard to plan with your friends?

Well, then, here's . . .

Another Twist on Fun

The fact is, adults can learn a lot about having fun from kids. If you really want to try something different, you might want to gather up a child or two in your extended family. This is more than baby-sitting. It can be an event that's special for you and special for the niece, nephew, or friend's child whom you take along.

Here are some great events for the kids and you to do together:

■ Special museums. Many cities now have a Please-Touch Museum—a masterpiece of child-centered design. You can gawk at a dinosaur, pat a boa constrictor, or banter with a parrot. Practically every city now has science and natural history museums specifically designed for children.

■ Zoos and nature centers. Children always enjoy live animals, and most cities have a children's zoo where they can touch the animals as well as see them. Plan on lunch.

■ Special playgrounds and amusement parks. Sometimes, parents have already promised to take their children to a playground or amusement park, then postpone the event. Check with the parents to find out what's been promised and where the child would like to go. (Peer pressure, even at the kindergarten level, may determine which park or playground the child wants to visit.)

■ Special rides and lunches. For a child of three or four, going on a bus or train and eating in a restaurant can be a great adventure.

■ Concerts, movies, shows. In Truffaut's film *Small Change,* there's a spectacular scene where kids are watching the marionette show in the Luxembourg Garden. While the Punch and Judy show is going on, Truffaut's camera turns to look at the children's faces—enraptured, suffused with enchantment. When you go to a children's show, get a seat near the front. Then, during the performance, turn around and look at the children behind you—laughing, scared, amazed, entranced. That's where the real show is.

■ Fairs and block parties. Just being with children helps you see the performances, contests, and exhibits through their eyes.

■ Parades. If parades have lost their charm for you, try taking a child along. The experience can make you instantly younger—and more aware.

■ Sports. Most children are pleased to find an adult who will throw a baseball, kick a soccer ball, play badminton, go swimming, ride bikes, or take them skating or sledding. If the child lives nearby, it is easy to set up an appointment that will take only an hour or two.

Privileged Position

Like grandparents, singles are in a privileged position vis-à-vis the children who belong to friends or relatives. You can be with the child for a short time, have a lot of fun yourself, and still leave the hard parts to the parents.

Because you are the older person who takes the child interesting places, you may be able to maintain your privileged position even into the teen years. Your relationship will change, of course, to meet the child on his or her own level.

Chapter 10

Getting Closer to Friends Who Have Partners

Couples tend to do things with other couples. Practically every single person has had the experience of "losing" a good friend to a marriage or intense relationship. Your friend is not really lost, of course, but sometimes it seems that way. Months go by without hearing from him or her. What happened? How could what appeared to be a close friendship evaporate so quickly?

"I find I have to work very hard at staying in touch with my married friends," Barbara told me. A college professor who was divorced three years ago, Barbara said she let her own friendships slide when she was married. "When you're in a relationship, you tend to do things with other couples. You *want* to keep your single friends, but somehow it's just not as easy.

"I know I'm the one who has to do the calling. And I have to be persistent—'Well, if not this week, how about next week?' It doesn't bother me if I have to keep at it. When I value a friendship, I want to keep it going."

Barbara finds that friends who are married will invite her to their homes, and she invites them to hers. "But they rarely ask me to go out with them," she adds. "If they're going out, they either go with other couples or by themselves."

On the other hand, Barbara is completely open to inviting one or both partners in a couple to go out with her to dinner, a game, or a show. "I invite my friend to go along with me. It's up to her whether she wants to invite her husband, and of course it's up to him whether he would like to go. But I do not feel obliged to find a date for myself just because there might be two of them and one of me."

Barbara is determined to maintain friendships that are meaningful to her. She does not always succeed in staying in touch with every friend. Some get wrapped up in their relationships or in family life. In these cases, Barbara lets the friendship run its course. "My true friends will continue to call. I know from experience that you can really lose out if you let go of your friends. I've also had friends reconnect when their marriages ended."

Inviting Couples

Inviting married friends to your house is good policy for a number of reasons. First, it convinces them (in case there's any doubt) that you like to be with them both—not just the person who is your closer friend.

Secondly, it gives you a chance to use your skills as a host or hostess. This is particularly important if you have been invited to their house for dinners, cocktail parties, or other social occasions. After all, why can't they be just as comfortable in your home as you are in theirs?

Thirdly, you keep the door open for reciprocation—and thus increase the invitations you're likely to receive.

Inviting Children

If the couple has children, they might like to bring them along. Working parents, especially, often don't get as much time with their children as they would like. And finding a sitter can be a problem. Invite the children as an option, and let the couple decide whether they want to bring them along.

David is a sculptor and silversmith who has a house and studio in suburban Philadelphia. Gail, an editor, and her husband, John, a landscape designer, both knew David in college. All three continued to see each other after Gail and John were married.

John and Gail now have two children. After the second came along, David realized that it was more up to him if they were to keep in touch, since John's and Gail's realities had changed.

I thought I would never see them again after the first was born [said David]. Their lives were preoccupied with baby rattles and changing diapers. Then I realized that their lives were just full to the brim. They were both working, they both had social obligations connected with their work, and when they got home, there were two kids at their heels demanding quality time.

I realized if we were going to get together, it was probably up to me to arrange it. I decided to include the kids as well. So I have the whole family over for a very simple dinner. Gail and John love it because they don't have to cook and clean up. I enjoy seeing them, even with the background noise.

Children require some special preparation, however. For young children, from toddlers to six- and seven-year-olds, consider:

- **Early hours.** A late night at your house can spell disaster for the parents the next morning, when they have to get up and deal with cranky children. Find out what time the children eat, so you can serve them at their normal hour. Expect that the parents will want to leave early.
- **Special food.** Some children simply will not eat many dishes you would prepare for company. Ask their parents what they *will* eat (which may be quite simple), then have it ready for them.
- **A separate table.** If a number of children are eating together, it's probably a good idea to have a low table with a few small chairs. Or let them eat at the kitchen table while the adults eat in the dining room.
- **A toy area.** Ask the parents to bring some favorites along.
- **A baby-sitter.** A sitter is optional, of course, but recommended if the children are toddlers or younger. Let the sitter arrive about a half-hour after the family, then monitor the children through dinner and playtime afterward. That will give their parents a break, and give you some time to catch up.

Older children might enjoy movies on video, music, and games. Some parents prefer to have their older children stay at the table. But other parents are pleased if you can offer their children the option of retreating to a game room or bedroom to pursue their own entertainments. Of course, if you have children of your own, you will include them in your plans for the evening.

The Drop-In Call

Keep your married friends on your birthday and holiday calendar! Even if you have not heard from them for a while, you can always send them a birthday gift or something special for the holidays. Remind your friends that you're thinking of them.

If the friendship begins to seem like a one-way street, all giving and no receiving, give it time. True friends will reciprocate when they can. The friendship might have to go through a period of change and adjustment when the other person gets married or begins a family. But by keeping in touch, usually the other person will see that you value the friendship and will make it continue.

When the Significant Other Is Standing in the Way

Lucille was having trouble with her friend's new husband. "I really don't enjoy spending time with Tina when Chuck is there," she said. "But on the other hand, I don't see why he should get in the way of my friendship with Tina."

After talking over some alternatives, Lucille decided the best approach was simply to invite Tina to lunch.

Later, when Tina's husband was out of town, Lucille and Tina got together for dinner and a play. They did a couple of Saturday-afternoon shopping trips together. Now, between lunches, shopping, and an occasional evening, the two friends continue to see each other frequently.

There was also a side benefit: once Lucille felt she could comfortably see Tina by herself from time to time, it was much easier to be around Chuck. Instead of someone who was blocking a friendship, he was simply part of her friend's life. Lucille found him much easier to accept in that role.

When You Decide It's Not Worth Pursuing

Time passes. Friends change. Friendships, like romantic relationships, can run their course.

If you find that the responsibility for maintaining the friendship is totally on your shoulders, it might be time to let go. When the other person is totally caught up in a relationship, a marriage, or family life and doesn't have time for friends, you may be causing yourself unnecessary pain or discomfort by putting your energy into trying to maintain something that is not going to work for either of you.

What are the signs that the friendship may have run its course?

■ *You have less to talk about when you are together.* If the other person only talks about his or her mate or new friends, and you no longer share common interests, it may be that the friendship is over.

■ *Invitations are not returned.* Couples *do* develop new circles of friends. They get caught up in social obligations. Prior friendships can be forgotten or set aside. Short of inviting yourself, there's very little you can do to correct this situation.

■ *The other person will not go anywhere without their mate.* This may be fine if you feel close to both of them. But if you are in a situation like Lucille's, where you feel uncomfortable with your friend's mate, it's unlikely you will want to spend much time with both of them.

■ *The other person becomes a matchmaker . . . when you don't want a match.* Those caught up in a relationship may begin to see matchmaking or marriage as the chosen way. (This usually wears off after time, but can be annoying while it lasts.) It could hurt your friendship if the other person is constantly reminding you that there's something wrong with you *as you are* and doesn't listen to your feedback.

■ *Your friend's mate sees you as a threat to the relationship.* If your friend's mate is jealous of you or overly insecure and possessive, those feelings are sure to have an impact on your friendship. You may be putting your friend in a very difficult position if you try to ignore the dynamics of the relationship. Suspicion and jealousy create the worst possible environment for a friendship. Rather than cause undue pain on all sides, you might choose to withdraw until the issues in the marriage or relationship have been resolved.

Losing a friend to a relationship can be all the more painful because it is usually so unnecessary. If the person is someone you truly value as a friend, however, then the loss of friendship is more likely to be temporary than final. By keeping in touch in small ways, you keep the door open. The time may come when, once again, you may be a very important person in that friend's life.

Unlikely as it may seem when you feel you are losing a friend, it is important to keep in mind that you are both growing. And, in time, you may grow close to each other again.

Chapter 11

Reaching Out to Former Friends

Jack is a graduate of the University of Colorado, where he was a runner, a member of the debating team, and a class vice-president. He is now municipal administrator in a medium-sized city where he has a large network of friends.

"There was one group in my class that was very close," he says. "We have continued to stay in touch and we see each other often. If I had to move right now, I might feel differently about being single. But with so many friends close by, I don't even think about getting out or trying to meet new people. It just happens."

Where are your college classmates? For that matter, what has become of your prep or high school friends? Finding out could be fairly simple and bring great rewards.

Often, friends from high school and college have some experiences that parallel your own. They are living through the same times, facing similar choices in their lives, and quite possibly feeling the same pressures. Their experiences in education, jobs, and relationships may be very close to yours. Why not look them up?

Class Reunions

The most obvious way to get in touch with former classmates is by going to class reunions. It's fun to find out what's happened to people. Almost every class has its share of surprises (the class nerd who became a heavy-duty financier, the silent girl with glasses and stringy hair who became a socialite, etc.).

But there is another kind of surprise that can await you in a class reunion. You may discover how you looked to others back then—and you get a clearer picture of who you are now. It is somewhat like returning to a small town where people know you. Just by talking to them, you can see how your views and expectations have changed.

Recently, I interviewed Carol, a woman who had just returned from her college class's fifteenth reunion. In college, she had belonged to a sorority for a while, but had dropped out during her senior year. Carol had kept in touch with some of these friends, but there were others she had not seen since graduation.

"It was fantastic," she told me. "It was like we'd been riding the same train for the past fifteen years. We could almost finish sentences for each other. I felt more in common with those people fifteen years *out* of school that I'd ever felt *in* school."

Since the reunion, she has become very close to one of her classmates who is now a music teacher and composer. They took a vacation together to Salzburg, and they have kept up a steady correspondence.

Alumni Associations

If you ever wonder what's become of a former classmate, there is a way to find out: get in touch with your alumni association. The association should have a list of most recent addresses. Or check the listings in class announcements, which appear at the back of many alumni magazines. If someone is listed whom you are interested in seeing, write or call the office for more information.

The other way is to ask around among your friends until you get a lead. If that person's name occurred to you, it was probably for a reason. By making a real effort, you probably will succeed.

If you have moved a lot and the alumni magazine hasn't caught up with you, be sure to send your address to the office. To let others in your class know about you, write an update on your moves, your career, and your status. You may be surprised at the people who want to get in touch with *you!*

Letter-Writing

Letter-writing is almost a lost art, but it shouldn't be! A letter to a friend you haven't seen for a long time can be a good way to break the ice. You do not have to apologize for not writing or not being in touch. People will usually welcome hearing from you.

On the other hand, do not take it personally if the recipient doesn't respond right away. People are busy, and many do not answer their correspondence immediately. Once you have opened the door with a letter, you might have to follow up with a phone call at some point.

When someone moves closer to you, it is an excellent excuse to get in touch. In your first letter, suggest getting together.

Even if years have gone by, let your letter melt them away. These friends are irreplaceable.

Christmas/Holiday Lists

Around December, the cards start coming in. They may be a reminder of all the people with whom you *didn't* get in touch during the year. Still, it doesn't hurt to save cards, names, and addresses.

A card may jog your memory about that person. In the next few weeks or months, you might find that you want to contact them. Also, having a list on file for *next* year makes the task of sending cards all that much easier when you have to face it.

Other Links

A fleeting acquaintance with someone outside high school or college can be renewed with a similar kind of letter. If you think about it, you will probably realize that there are some people you have met in the past whom you might like to see again. Among them:

- Someone you met on vacation
- A former business associate who has changed companies or moved away
- Someone you met at a conference
- A romantic relationship that might now work as a friendship
- The person you talked to at a party. (Can't recall a last name or find an address? Check your file of business cards—or call the person who held the party!)

- Someone you met at the health club or at a sporting event
- Someone you met at a singles event

There's no time limit on a possible friendship. You have nothing to lose, and everything to gain, by getting in touch with someone who interested you at one time, even if you met that person months or years ago. Whether you were just attracted to that person for an hour, an evening, or a weekend, the possibility of an ongoing friendship is still there.

Why not explore it further?

Chapter 12

Getting Involved in Good Causes and Community Activities

In a large city, you may find two or three hundred organizations that constantly need volunteers, ranging from hospitals and libraries to day-care centers, environmental groups, and youth services. If you want to work close to home, your neighborhood, block, or condominium association may have immediate need for your short-term services. On a national scale, political parties are looking for volunteers in every area from stamping envelopes to writing press releases; from canvassing neighborhoods to making important logistical arrangements.

As a socializing strategy, volunteer work is a good way to meet people who are working for a common cause. But other criteria are useful: will the work still be satisfying, even if you don't make a lot of friends?

Give yourself a head start by evaluating what you would like to get out of this kind of work and how much time you can put into it. If you work full days with regular hours, some volunteer programs will be out of the question. But there are many ways you can help after hours, or work on short-term projects during weekends and vacations.

Here are just some of the ways you can assist:

- *In the community.* Fund-raising, community research and surveys, and business aid. This is a great way to get to know your neighbors and to find out what the issues are in your immediate neighborhood. If you have experience in communications, planning, finances, or organization, you could be a valuable player.
- *In the classroom.* There are many adult education courses, and you may be eligible to teach one in your area of expertise. Preparation may be minimal, if you already know the subject area, and you are meeting people who have an interest in what you're talking about. If your background is in music, art, or theater, you might be able to participate in teaching programs in the schools (some of these posts carry a stipend). If you want to work with youth, you can do one-on-one tutoring. Many literacy programs need your help!
- *In health-care facilities.* Your help is needed in working with the emotionally ill, with alcoholic and drug-addicted patients, and in family-planning clinics. You will also get to know your support group well as you work together and form friendships. Volunteers also answer hotlines, help with rehabilitation programs, and assist in fund-raising and community services.
- *Help for the aging.* Many aged people who live at home count on daily visits from Meals on Wheels. You can provide companionship to people who are bedridden, write letters for them, assist with social activities, or read to the blind. Those who are homebound may need occasional transportation. A few minutes of conversation can mean a great deal. You are a special visitor who brings news of the outside world; if you

can visit at regular intervals, your visits will be eagerly anticipated.

■ *Legal rights and crime prevention.* Work in a program to improve police-community relations, or a probation program to help former prisoners return to the community. You can also do pro bono work, providing legal or social services, if you are an attorney or counselor.

■ *Social support services.* In this area, your opportunities range from counseling young people in career planning to investigating offenses against fair-housing laws and facilitating tenant-landlord relationships. In addition, volunteers are often needed for distribution of food or clothing, working with groups to improve interracial relations, and operating volunteer centers.

■ *Political.* Activities range from voter registration to lobbying, petitioning, and proposing legislation. In addition to political party work, consider nonaligned political action for advocacy groups or peace organizations.

■ *Environmental.* You have your choice of local, regional, or national environmental groups. At the local level, you may be able to help with recycling, restoring land use, contributing to conservation education, and creating playgrounds and parks. At the regional level, there are groups working for the preservation of parks and opposing the destruction of the environment. Nationally, groups ranging from Greenpeace to the Sierra Club mount campaigns, sponsor special causes, and lobby vigorously. Individuals who contribute their time and energy help make the campaign successful.

Volunteer Work Is Not Missionary Work!

With a wide selection of organizations and causes from which to choose, you have many options. You have the opportunity to select work that will reward you personally while also making a contribution to the community, the environment, or the quality of life. This is not a lifelong commitment. You can volunteer for hours, days, or years: it all depends on how much you like what you are doing and how much you enjoy the people you work with. Also, volunteer work offers many persons an opportunity to work on different kinds of projects and wield a greater degree of authority than their regular jobs afford them. It can be a great change of pace for that reason alone.

The experience will be most rewarding if you *do* have a clear idea of the rewards that mean most to you. Do you like to help people who are sick or in need? Or would you rather be involved with young, active, idealistic people who are working for a cause? Do you enjoy the gradual rewards of seeing a student begin to comprehend what's written on the printed page? Or would you rather campaign actively for fair housing and decent schools?

You are most likely to continue doing that which rewards you. So, in the long run, both you and the organization you work for are better off if you do something that provides you with selfish as well as altruistic rewards.

Almost any kind of volunteer work should begin with a probationary period during which you meet people, find out what work is involved, and find out what your role is. If volunteer work does not look promising, you can always drop it. But if the work provides its own rewards, you may discover a long-term commitment that adds a different dimension to your life and is very fulfilling.

Chapter 13

Getting More Enjoyment Out of Vacations

Vacations offer great opportunities for socializing, depending on the kind of vacation you choose. To help you evaluate some of your many choices, just consider:

- Do you want to travel to some exotic place with a tour group?
- Would you like to lie on the beach, bask in the sun, and have someone deliver piña coladas to your hand?
- Is this vacation an opportunity to meet new people or to travel with friends?
- Are you looking for scenery, exercise, and a healthful atmosphere?
- Do you want parties, entertainment, and luxuries to pamper yourself with?
- Do you prefer familiar surroundings where you can get away from it all and enjoy the small pleasures?

Your Agenda

Whatever vacation you choose, it is important to go with your own agenda.

Shelly, a thirty-four-year-old dental assistant, told me:

> The worst vacation I ever had was at a Club Med. The best vacation I ever had was at a Club Med. When I went the first time, I was looking for romance. I went with the idea I had to meet somebody. Surprise—the only guys I met were trying to hit on someone fast, and those were the guys I least wanted to be with. I put myself in a double bind.
>
> When I went back to Club Med again, I said to myself, "I don't care who I meet, I'm going to have a good time." So of course I met people. Not necessarily anyone I wanted to be romantically involved with, people who were just really nice. I've been back several times since, always with that attitude, and I've had some very special kinds of experiences.

If you are open to *any* kind of socializing—not just meeting someone special—you have numerous opportunities to meet people while you travel. Shelly has found that she enjoys planning a trip as much as getting there. When she plans to visit a country, she reads up on it before going and learns some of the language. Traveling with a tour group, she recently took a trip to China that she calls "the vacation of a lifetime." Again, she had her own agenda. She traveled with the group, enjoyed their company, and had the opportunity to explore a country she had always wanted to see.

Going with Friends

Blake is a forty-three-year-old executive who travels a great deal on business and pleasure. He told me:

It doesn't appeal to me to go on a vacation by myself. Usually, when I go on vacations, I go with someone else—and often it's somebody who lives out of town. Last year, I met a good, close friend of mine in Orlando, and we spent a week at Disney World.

I went to Seattle by myself, but I also have many friends there. And when I go to Hartford, I usually stay with friends. I can't remember ever just going on a vacation by myself and returning by myself without knowing somebody at my destination. I always make arrangements with somebody there ahead of time.

That even goes for sports that I like a lot—like skiing. I would never go to a ski resort just to stand in a lift line and do the trails by myself. I get in with a group. For me, getting to a place and socializing is an important part of the vacation.

If meeting friends is important to you, let your friends know where you would like to take a vacation—and what your plans are. A vacation gives you an excellent opportunity to hook up with somebody who lives far away and to do things you enjoy doing together—whether skiing, hiking, sailing, exploring, or any other activity or entertainment.

If you can visit a friend on his or her home turf, you have the advantage of also meeting *that* person's circle of friends. Your coming to town may be your friend's excuse to have a party, see an opening, or go to a show or game.

Relaxing, Rewarding, and Healthful Retreats

Connie and Rita take a vacation together every year. Connie's family has a house in Boca Raton, and Rita has an open invitation to visit whenever Connie goes there. "I haven't missed a year since college," Rita told me. "I do lots of swimming. We play tennis. I catch up on my reading and sunbathing, and just mellow out."

If you don't have a friend with a house in Florida, there are other ways you can take relaxing, rewarding, and healthful vacations that offer opportunities for socializing. Among them:

- *Health spas.* Choose a beautiful location that comes highly recommended. In most spas, you are expected to follow a strict diet-and-exercise routine. But you have ample opportunities to meet people at meals, during walks, or in the exercise areas.
- *Special-purpose retreats.* Many kinds of workshops are held at camps and retreats throughout the country. You can choose one on the basis of friends' recommendations, location, or personal interest. Some workshops specialize in personal growth; others in spirituality, adult transitions, body movement, massage, yoga, or stress reduction. Socializing comes during the workshops, during meals, or in various group activities.
- *Religious retreats.* Most religious organizations sponsor weekend or week-long retreats. The group may be all-male, all-female, or mixed. While some religious retreats are structured around a theme or discussion topic, there is always time for socializing.
- *Outdoor adventure tours.* The outdoor travel business is booming, and a greater variety of tours is available now than ever before. You can take a ship to Antarctica, travel by horseback through Mongolia,

go whitewater rafting through the Grand Canyon, or sail the Aegean. Everyone you meet will have at least one thing in common: a taste for the same type of adventure.

- *Cruises.* Some cruises are expressly designed for singles or have a special singles package deal. If you like the atmosphere of a cruise, this is a wonderful opportunity to socialize and meet new people. A luxury liner is a superb getaway. All your needs are catered to, and you can set your own pattern of activity (or inactivity).

(For more suggestions on vacation plans, see Part Three, page 202.)

Chapter 14

Good Ideas for Weekends and Holidays

Strategies for holidays are among the most difficult for some singles. Many couples and families make their plans early. If you have a tradition of joining your parents or close relatives for the holidays, it could be difficult to break with that. If you want to include people in your holiday plans—or get them to include you—then you need to make arrangements well in advance.

If you find that a parent or both parents expect you to show up automatically, let them know your plans as early as possible

Holiday Strategies

If you decide to enjoy the holidays in your own home, this is an excellent time for planning a social event with other single friends or couples.

Here are some ideas:

■ Have an open house in the afternoon during holidays such as Christmas, New Year's Day, Valentine's

Day, Easter, Memorial Day, the Fourth of July, or Labor Day. Consider a joint party with other friends, using the most suitable home for the event.

- Make plans to join another couple or family, or have them over.
- If doing good for others makes you feel good, think about giving some time to others less fortunate than you. For instance, you may want to visit a nursing home, a hospital, or a center for the homeless.

Weekends

Socializing on weekends can become a comfortable habit if you want it to be. A woman who called in to my radio show suggested to my listeners:

Give yourself two assignments during the week. Say to yourself, "Okay, I will make plans for Saturday night, and I will invite someone to brunch on Sunday morning." When you meet people during the week, say to yourself, "I wonder what this person's doing Saturday night. I wonder what they're doing Sunday morning."

I don't find it easy to reach out and invite people to do things. But I know I'll just have a much more pleasant weekend if I make appointments to see people or do things on Saturday and Sunday.

Several listeners in the audience thanked the caller for her suggestion. One woman noted:

I think I got out of the habit of thinking it was *my* responsibility to ask someone out. In college, I remember women sitting around the dorm on Saturday night because they didn't have a date. I have friends who are still doing that today. You wait for people to invite you to do things. When they don't, you wonder what's wrong with you. That just doesn't make sense.

It *is* up to you. If you know you have a self-commitment to direct your social activities on the weekend, you can take care of that assignment a week or two ahead. Whether you are planning for weekends, holidays, vacations, or social occasions, you are your own best social director.

Chapter 15

How to Start Socializing

"I'm afraid I won't know what to say."

From time immemorial, friendships, meetings, greetings, and untold opportunities have been stalled by that single, most prevalent fear. But there's probably more to it than that. Many people are afraid that what they *do* say will make them sound silly, inappropriate, uneducated, or just plain out of it.

The most effective ways to break through are often the simplest ways. The great secrets of social success have more to do with attitude than with native charm, wit, and wisdom. As one hostess told me, "There are three things I always do. I smile. I look the other person in the eye. And I never try to be clever."

This is an approach that has worked for her—has made it easy for her to socialize. You might choose a different approach that would work equally well. But whatever you do, remember that your words don't matter as much as your attitude:

- Do you *want* to meet the other person?
- Are you truly *interested*?
- Do you want to get to know that person better?

If your answers to these three questions are "Yes," then you will probably *find* a way to have a conversation with that person. Even if that person is shy or is distracted by other people, your interest is likely to win out.

How to Start a Conversation

One way to start a conversation is by asking questions related to the situation:

At a party: "How long have you known Richard and Gail [the host and hostess]?"

In a classroom: "What do you know about our teacher?"

In a ticket line: "What have you heard about this show?"

To a neighbor: "When is the block party? Has it been announced yet?"

You can also start conversations by talking about the other person. Often you can begin with a comment and then ask a question. Since most people like to talk about themselves, you will usually get a positive response from a complimentary or interested observation:

"Those are great-looking shoes. Where did you find them?"

"Lorrie tells me you like to travel. What are your plans this year?"

"I heard you say you have your pilot's license. How long have you been flying?"

"I noticed you were looking at that print. What do you think of it?"

Once the other person is talking, he or she will probably show a greater willingness to make self-disclosures if you are willing to disclose *yourself.* You can promote self-disclosure by revealing facts, opinions, and information. But if you can also reveal some *feelings,* people will know you are able to warm up to them and to reach out.

At the *first* level of self-disclosure, you might give information like:

- Your name
- Your occupation
- Facts about where you live and what you do every day
- Opinions about public personalities or a news item
- Observations about people or events

But if you want to take the conversation to *another* level of self-disclosure, there's much more you can add:

- Information about your background, your friends, your education, and your family
- Discussion of times when you have felt excitement, joy, sorrow, happiness, or pain
- Experiences related to winning, losing, dealing with difficult problems, or trying something for the first time
- Your likes and dislikes regarding personalities and events
- Observations about where you are now in your career or personal life—and where you hope to be in the future

Of course, you might not feel comfortable with a greater degree of self-disclosure on first meeting. But

remember, as you disclose more about yourself, you
will probably find that the other person will offer an
equal amount of self-disclosure. Balanced self-disclosure is a good way to keep a conversation moving,
to create interest, and encourage openness on both
sides.

Do You Want to Socialize?

I generally encourage my clients to take risks. I
might ask them to assign themselves specific challenges, such as: "At the next party, I will to come away
with the names and telephone numbers of three people
I've never met before."

At first, an assignment like this might seem intimidating to Joan, especially if she thinks of herself as
being a shy, quiet, or introverted person. But what is a
likely scenario if she *does* approach new people at a
party? Joan realizes that nothing catastrophic will happen. No one is going to shout at her or tell her to go
away. At worst, she might get the cold shoulder from
someone.

We review what she might do if the worst does
happen—what if she *does* get the cold shoulder? How
will she feel? How can she *keep going* so she will come
back from the party with the names and telephone
numbers of three new people?

If Joan says she will feel "awful" or "horrible," I
encourage her to replace those words with other, less
catastrophic descriptions. Certainly it would be *unfor-
tunate* if someone gave her the cold shoulder. She
might feel *uncomfortable*. But it wouldn't be the end of
the world. After all, that other person doesn't even
know Joan. So the fact that the person is cold or rude
really has nothing to do with her personally.

What will happen to *you* if you encounter rejection of some kind?

If you have given yourself an assignment to meet three new people, you can't let one rejection stop you. You have to move on. You have set yourself up for success. You *will* meet new people, and in the process, you will end up knowing a little bit about each one of them. And the more you disclose about yourself, the better they will know you.

Best of all, if you do meet rejection at some point, you will discover that you can live through it without crumbling. You have the inner resources to pull through!

So once you have made an assignment to yourself, don't stop until you have completed it. You will come away knowing that, no matter what happens, you can accomplish what you set out to do in a social situation. You can decide how you want to behave, and you have some control over the outcome. Most important, you can count on yourself to fulfill the assignment that you make for *yourself!*

Respecting Your Comfort Zone

I find that people sometimes think too much in terms of exotic things to do in order to meet people. You don't *have* to be daring or exotic! (In fact, if you're not by nature a daring, exotic person, you don't gain anything by pretending to be.) Why not look for creative solutions that are within your comfort zone? Try answering these questions in your notebook:

- What do I *like* to do?
- What's *fun* for me?
- Where do I feel secure and safe with people?

If you feel you are spending too much time alone, then you know you have to make a conscious effort to expand your comfort zone. On the other hand, if the time alone is time that you cherish and value, you certainly don't have an *obligation* to socialize. As one client expressed it, "I see singlehood as a luxury. There are times when I like to be alone, but I find I have to defend that right. When people say, 'Well, why *can't* you do this?' you might have to say, 'I'd rather be alone.' *You have to defend the right to be by yourself.*"

Stages of Socializing

In meeting people and socializing, we often have to strike a balance between taking risks and feeling secure. What if you have social needs that aren't being met? What if the inner voice that is your social director won't *tell* you what to do? Sometimes, it's just a matter of getting started. If you take the first step, the rest becomes easier.

Here are the ways some people have done it in the past:

JACLYN

"I started contra-dancing with a beginners' group that was meeting at the high school on Thursday nights. In contra-dancing, you're always changing partners and learning new steps. It's very entertaining. I loved the dancing, there was wine afterwards, and I got talking to some people . . ."

GREG

"I joined a mixed volleyball team. Some men and women in my firm wanted to start a team. As it turned out, there's a mixed volleyball league in the city, so we play against other firms. In the past six months, I would say I've met more men *and* women because of that volleyball team than I did in the past six years . . ."

PATRICIA

"I went to a benefit sponsored by my alumnae association. There were only two other people from my class, but we really were glad to see each other. One of the women was new to the area. The other had been here awhile. We started talking about things to do, and I realized that there was really a lot I hadn't explored yet. We started making plans . . ."

CALLIE

"I went to one of those motivational seminars. It was a three-day course, and I was very skeptical at first. You know—'How is this going to change me?' Well, I don't know whether it changed me or not, but there was a group of us there who seemed to be going through *exactly* the same kinds of experiences in our lives. After the seminar was over, we had a celebration. I thought, I really want to see these people again. So we made plans . . ."

PHIL

"I'm your basic recluse, and I don't go for parties. But since I'm a freelance designer, I do a lot of my work alone. I wanted something I could do with people in a kind of nonsocial situation, but where we might get talking. I didn't want great conversation, just good company. I read that the art museum was looking for some skilled volunteers to do restoration work. Twice a week I go down there, work with four or five other people. I might have coffee or a drink afterward with someone, but some nights we just work away. That's fine. It can be very satisfying . . ."

KENDRA

"I had twenty people over to my apartment. It was a catered dinner with invitations. I was worried. First I thought no one would show up. Then, when they showed up, I thought they would be bored. I thought the dinner would be a disaster. But it wasn't. People warmed up, it turned into a real party. Believe it or not, I'd never done that before, not just for myself. It was a breakthrough . . ."

What's Right for You?

Look at the socializing strategies you prioritized by number at the beginning of this section. Now is the time to begin making plans. Whom would you like to call tomorrow? What information do you need about organizations or activities? Who can help you? What will you say to people you meet for the first time? How do you visualize your social life six months from now?

Part of good socializing is using your imagination to create the kind of social life you imagine for yourself. You have the opportunity to do something, tomorrow, that you have never done before. You can meet people whom you didn't know yesterday. They, in turn, will be the key to future contacts . . . and a better social life.

Next time your social director (you) whispers a suggestion in your ear, listen! The best strategies are the ones you believe in—and the ones that work for you. But you'll never know whether they do work until you try. And only the person in the mirror can get you to do that.

Part Two

Why No One Has to Be Lonely

A major part of the art of living single is the art of not being lonely. Of course, being lonely is not unique to singles life. People in marriages and relationships can be just as lonely as those who are unattached.

For example, one married woman said to me: "We sit across from one another at breakfast and I think to myself, Who is he? I don't know him at all. We're complete strangers."

Her husband told me (separately): "I don't really have any friends. I'm not really close to anyone I work with. My wife has her own life. The kids are caught up in what they're doing. I guess that's just the way it is."

Loneliness has many different forms and dimensions. There are people who are extremely depressed when they are feeling lonely. Their thoughts and feelings run in cycles of self-doubt and self-blaming. Their lives become filled with desperation and anguish. For some, being alone seems like the cause of loneliness. Yet for someone else the same solitude might lead to growth, renewal, and self-expression. Why do the qualities of aloneness become a creative force in one person and yet lead to self-destructive influences in another?

Loneliness has different meanings. It often means *missing someone*. That someone could be a friend, or a person you fell in love with, or someone you once were married to. Sometimes, any reminder of that person's not being there becomes painful.

But sometimes there is a longing that has nothing to do with a *particular* person. It's a longing for somebody—anybody. As many single people have told me, "I'd just like to have someone there when I wake up in the morning."

One single woman: "I really want someone at the end of a terrible day. When I come in the door, there should be someone there when I say, 'Things are a mess and I feel crummy.'"

Another woman: "Sunday morning is when I miss having *someone*. You know. Just to have him there with me, reading the Sunday paper."

Loneliness can also result from a whole host of longings—longing for warmth, a longing to be held, to be comforted, a longing for companionship, for conversation, for stimulation, for contentment.

In addition, loneliness masquerades in feelings, memories, wishes, expectations, dreams, and escapes. Loneliness can be an energizing motivator or a whirlpool of despair. Escape from loneliness can be an exhilarating liberation; its return can cause anger, resentment, and fear. Some people come to know loneliness well: though never welcoming it, they learn to acknowledge it and leave it behind. To others, it's an unwelcome, fearful guest.

Loneliness takes so many forms because it's often a reflection of us. It's influenced by our past and present lives, our friends, spouses, and lovers, our hopes, our disappointments, and our world.

There are ways to conquer loneliness. You can be alone without feeling lonely. But, ultimately, how you experience aloneness—as loneliness or as solitude—is influenced and directed by the way you see yourself.

Chapter 16

Attitudes About Loneliness

Although loneliness is different for everyone, there are times when feelings of loneliness are most common to single people.

■ *After hours.* Katrina is a senior nurse in a medical center:

I'm very close to the people I work with. But I'm the only single woman on staff. At work, we're all together, we're equals. I talk about my life; they talk about theirs. Then every once in a while it hits me: it's different for them. When they leave work, they'll go home to their houses, their husbands . . . and, now, some of them have children. That doesn't really bother me. It just hits me sometimes. They have something I don't have.

■ *Weekends.* Norman, a forty-seven-year-old social worker:

Weekends are not especially hard. I find things to do and people to connect with. I'm very much a people person, though I like to spend time reading—and walking, too. But it sometimes gets bad in the early hours of the morning, when I first wake up. The worst time is Monday morning—the Monday morning blues. Or on a Sunday afternoon, if I'm not with someone.

■ *Holidays.* A thirty-seven-year-old attorney, Sarah recalled her fear of being alone on holidays:

I remember in graduate school, one time, everyone went home for the holidays and I stayed. I was dating someone at the time, but one of his best friends had just died, so my boyfriend was away at the funeral. I was feeling terribly lonely. I threw myself into work. I did a whole semester's work by midterm. It made me feel better because I felt that I was accomplishing something.

■ *During hard times.* Loren, thirty-four, a radio producer:

I had just been fired from my job. I had just broken up with someone. It was one of those times when everything just ends in your life. I said, "I've got to get away . . ."

■ *When you have unfulfilled romantic feelings.* Carla, a twenty-nine-year-old magazine writer:

Sometimes it does get to me, Dr. Broder. Sometimes I turn around and look at myself in the mirror and think that I'm fairly attractive, I'm fairly intelligent, I'm fairly independent, I'm educated, and I have an interesting career with a lot of travel. And I wonder, "What am I doing wrong that I'm not meeting someone?" But then I think, maybe it's not only me. Maybe it's the other per-

son who doesn't know how to give me a chance—
or how to give himself a chance to get to know me.

■ *On vacation.* Patty, who is forty-six, owns her
own travel agency and frequently travels by herself.

There have been times I've been so lonely I
wanted to do myself in. One night I was traveling
through Spain by myself. I was in Madrid and all
alone. The place where I was staying was terrible. I
was so lonely. I said, "I can't stand this. If I just sit
here I'll die." So I put on the one dynamite dress I
had with me, walked into the lobby of the best
hotel in Madrid, right into the middle of a big
wedding. There was this reception going on, everyone was very friendly, and I had a wonderful time.

■ *When you are reminded of someone you have lost
or left behind.* At thirty-six, Chris broke off his engage-
ment with a woman he had been seeing for five years.

It's particularly bad when you wake up at one
o'clock in the morning and you feel lonely and you
wonder, "Oh, my God, did I do the right thing
with the person I was with. Or should I reconsider?" You think, "I'm going to get old and not
have anybody around. I could get ill." You know,
you just want to have somebody to pour your
heart out to, who will unconditionally or almost
unconditionally accept you.

■ *When you can use some support.* At the time his
wife left him, Dennis, forty-six, was starting his own
business.

The stress was terrible. I was working eighteen
hours a day. Then I came home and there was no
one there. The loneliness got worse. I don't really
know what I wanted—just someone to be there
when I got home, I guess.

■ *When you believe that other people expect you to be with someone*. Lisa is a twenty-nine-year-old landscape designer:

> When I get the feeling that I don't want to be alone any more, most of it comes from the message that "You should be coupled and not uncoupled." I get a lot of that from my parents. But also, just everyday stuff reminds me: things are designed for people in relationships. It's easier to go out as a couple than as a single, and that message is pretty clear. When I get upset, it's brought on by those messages.

Powerful Illusions

For many people, bouts of loneliness are a fact of life. The only thing that can be said for certain is that it is normal to experience some loneliness, and that there is nothing abnormal about anyone who feels lonely sometimes. It is a part of the human condition that cannot be denied.

But, for each of us, there may be times when the feelings and longings that accompany those periods seem overwhelming. How we learn to cope with our loneliness is so personal, so private, so unique to our own way of looking at the world, ourselves, and other people, that it can take a lot of practice to get it right.

One of the most powerful illusions that we have when we are lonely is that we often feel we are completely alone in our loneliness. Maybe you tell yourself: "I am the only person who feels this way. Nobody else could feel like this. There's something wrong with me."

This illusion is reinforced by the fact that most people do *not* talk about their loneliness or admit that they are sometimes lonely. So we see images of people who

look successful, who appear happy, well-loved, surrounded by friends. Their happiness, their freedom
from pain, can seem very unavailable to us when loneliness hits. You may even long to *be* someone else, just
for a while, in the same way you may long for love or
companionship.

But almost everyone feels lonely sometimes. People
of high accomplishment are no exception:

Elizabeth Taylor, after the death of Mike Todd:

> I could not bear the loneliness of being without
> the man I really loved. I could not sleep, and as the
> weeks went by my insomnia grew worse. As a
> result, I began to take sleeping pills. It was the
> only way I knew to get up at 5 A.M. and not be a
> zombie. . . . My intense loneliness, combined
> with the nearness of someone [Eddie Fisher] who
> had been so close to my beloved made me suscep-
> tible. In hindsight, I know I wasn't thinking
> straight.
>
> (Elizabeth Taylor, *Elizabeth Takes Off.* New
> York: G. P. Putman's Sons, 1987.)

The late Dag Hammarskjöld, former Secretary General of the United Nations:

> Pray that your loneliness may spur you into
> finding something to live for, great enough to die
> for.
>
> (Leonard Safir and William Safire, comp., *Good
> Advice.* New York: Times Books, 1982.)

Henry Miller, to Anais Nin (August 23, 1933):

> I'm not unhappy. Nor am I happy. I'm just ex-
> tended—between places. . . . I'm lonely. . . . The
> main thing is to feel your presence—hear you
> humming or yawning, see your combs & brushes

lying around, worry about which dress you should put on, etc.

(*A Literate Passion:* Letters of Anaïs Nin and Henry Miller. Orlando, FL: Harcourt Brace Jovanovich, 1987.)

Emily Dickinson:

I fear this—is Loneliness—
The Maker of the Soul
Its Caverns and its Corridors
Illuminate—or seal—

(Thomas H. Johnson, ed., *The Complete Poems of Emily Dickinson.* Boston: Little Brown, 1960.)

Ingrid Bergman:

19 January 1935. My first opening night. . . . What would Mama and Papa have said if they could see me here in my loneliness. I long to creep into someone's arms to find protection and comfort and love.

(Ingrid Bergman and Alan Burgess, *Ingrid Bergman: My Story.* New York: Delacorte, 1980.)

Loneliness is something that each of these people, in their own way, came to terms with. Loneliness can be conquered. In fact, loneliness can spur us on the path to renewal and growth. "I never found the companion that was so companionable as solitude," wrote Thoreau in *Walden.* By making solitude a companion rather than loneliness an enemy, you open the possibility of finding something in yourself that can be creative and self-renewing.

Twenty-nine and recently divorced, Leslie was living alone for the first time in her life. She was wrestling with many issues of loneliness. During one conversation I had with her, she suddenly remembered a young man she had met briefly when she was driving cross-country with a friend. The young man had been traveling by bicycle, carrying only a backpack. He was all by himself.

At the time, Leslie had wondered how he could do it. She could not imagine why anyone would choose such a lonely way to travel.

The cyclist had described his trip to her as "the ultimate getting-away. I have complete freedom to go. Nobody's putting demands on me, and I'm not self-conscious about being alone."

That made an impression on Leslie, because she had never taken a vacation or gone anywhere by herself. This reluctance to travel by herself was really a fear that she would feel lonely and out of place wherever she went.

During the transition period that she was going through, we agreed to several assignments that might make Leslie feel better about being alone—and help her cope with loneliness. One assignment was to go to a restaurant and eat all by herself. Another was to go to a concert by herself. A third was to spend a day by herself in a crowded park.

Before and during each "assignment," she was to say to herself, "This is something that I have *chosen* to do by myself—not because I *have* to be alone."

With that affirmation, each assignment became for her a very positive experience. She realized that much of her discomfort about being alone had resulted from the feeling that people would notice she was all by herself. She didn't want them to think there was something wrong with her.

Also, she was inexperienced in going places by herself. But when she went alone by choice, her experiences gave her more confidence.

As she began to look for other things she could do by herself, she recalled how she had reacted to the young man cycling cross-country. At the time, it had seemed impossible that he could travel all alone without being lonely. But now that loneliness had ceased to be a threat to her, she understood why he would seek out the rewards of traveling alone. In fact, she began making plans to spend her next vacation by herself.

Alone, Not Lonely

Wonderful things are done by people alone. Some of the things we pursue in private can touch other lives. Others remain private pursuits (in some cases, private passions), when we are consumed with enjoying, thinking, creating.

Consider some of these enjoyable things that people can do when alone:

■ Many people visit art museums, galleries, and exhibitions when they are alone. The visual experience is something that you can enjoy completely by yourself.

■ Music, too, can be a very individual experience. There's no reason why you should not enjoy a rock concert, a symphony orchestra, or a night at the opera by yourself.

■ If you are someone who loves to read, every moment that you are alone becomes an opportunity to indulge, enjoy, and explore new books, new authors, and new ideas.

■ For someone who enjoys gardening, the hours alone in the garden are filled with rewards. If you take pleasure in working outdoors—planting, pruning, and watching things grow—a garden is an ever-changing source of interest.

■ If you ever wonder what you are thinking during your times alone—if you want to record thoughts, feelings, and impressions—a journal of self-exploration can take you deeply into your own reflections.

■ Playing with a pet can provide many moments of enjoyment when you are alone.

■ Or you may enjoy the time you spend by yourself organizing your living arrangements, dreaming up improvements, or deciding on colors, patterns, and new additions.

■ Thinking, just thinking, is a great journey we can take by ourselves. Whether you wish to philosophize, meditate, fantasize, or speculate, there is no limit to the exploration that the mind can take when you are alone.

■ Exercise does not have to be a group activity or team sport. Whether you prefer sports, calisthenics, or other kinds of recreation, there are many kinds of exercise that you can do alone.

■ Enjoy nature with a long walk through a bird sanctuary, a day by the seashore, or an afternoon hike. You don't need a companion: there are many things about nature that you will be likely to discover only if you are alone.

■ Numerous people have set out to meet challenges on their own, and the solitariness of their quest is an end and a purpose in itself. What does it feel like to conquer the ocean singlehandedly in a sailboat? To climb a sheer mountain? To write a long novel? When you discover the thrills of meeting such challenges and conquering the odds, you are likely to want more.

■ Traveling can be a lonely pursuit only if you feel lonely, but exhilarating and exciting if you *want* to travel alone and are eager to explore.

■ Investigating the unknown can be a singlehanded undertaking, sometimes frustrating but often more rewarding than you could imagine.

Enriching Your Time with People

The time that you spend alone does not make you into a "loner" who is unable to socialize.

On the contrary, the work, discoveries, and adventures you undertake by yourself can help you feel more connected with people and enrich your time with others.

When you get in touch with things that are most important and most meaningful to you during your time alone, you develop and deepen the interests that you can share with others. At many points in history, there have been exciting encounters among likeminded people working on isolated problems. Artists pursuing their solitary work experience bursts of inspiration and a cross-fertilization of ideas when they meet someone whose work bears some relationship to their own. People grappling privately with personal issues experience a strong group feeling when those issues are shared or expressed by others.

The hours alone are never wasted. They give us the power to grow, to enrich and broaden our experiences, to know many facets of ourselves that we may never have known before—and that, in turn, may give us the power to relate to people in many new ways.

Self-Assessment

If you have times when you feel lonely, you can change your attitude about being alone. It is possible to *look forward* to your alone time as a time of peaceful solitude. You can then find rewards.

The chart below shows two sets of contrasting attitudes. In Column A are the attitudes that lead to loneliness. In Column B are the attitudes that may help you enjoy solitude. If you identify an attitude in Column A that is close to an attitude that you share, look at the corresponding attitude in Column B. This second attitude is the affirmation that could be the key to helping you overcome loneliness.

ALTERNATIVE ATTITUDES

A. Attitudes That Lead to Loneliness	B. Attitudes That Help You Enjoy Solitude
The loneliness gets so bad that I don't know whether I will survive.	I have survived loneliness in the past, and *I know I can choose both to survive it and learn from it in the future.*
No matter how little or how much time I spend alone, it feels like too much.	I usually look forward to my time alone as a special opportunity for introspection.
Other people do not feel as lonely as I do.	I imagine that everyone feels lonely from time to time. Being lonely does not make me less of a person.
I regret many past actions that have led to my present lonely situation.	Dwelling on the past will get me nowhere, but I can refuse to be overcome by loneliness and choose to spend my time alone or with others.
If someone would only reach out to me, I would not feel so lonely.	Whenever I choose to, I can reach out to people as an alternative to being lonely.

Attitudes are learned. They're not something that we're born with. The good news is, since they *are* learned, you can change them. An attitude from Column B can resolve the problem based on Column A.

To help yourself do this, write down on a 3-by-5-inch index card at least one of the affirmations from Column B. Tape that card to the refrigerator or the car dashboard—wherever you might be when you begin to get those feelings. When you start feeling lonely or negative, look at that card and make that affirmation to yourself.

By adopting that positive affirmation, you have a powerful way to gain greater control over your attitudes.

Chapter 17

Being Alone Is Something to Explore!

Most people who excel relish their time alone as a time of creativity.

Ray Charles:

> If I went to a club, it was in the hopes of sitting in and maybe finding work. I always had a purpose and a motive. Loud parties, large crowds, being out with the gang—none of these things interested me. And the same's true today. I'm still alone.
>
> (Ray Charles, *Brother Ray: Ray Charles' Own Story*. New York: Dial Press, 1978.)

Albert Einstein:

> Although I am a typical loner in daily life, my consciousness of belonging to the invisible community of those who strive for truth, beauty, and justice has preserved me from feeling isolated.
>
> (James Sayen, *Einstein in America*. New York: Crown, 1985.)

Woody Allen:

Well, it has never really meant a thing to me what anyone said. I'm just sort of going the route I've chosen to go. If people like it, they like it, and if they don't, they don't.

(William E. Geist, "Woody Allen Talks." *Rolling Stone,* April 19, 1987, no. 497.

When people are totally caught up in their art, their thoughts, their work, their personal exploration, and aloneness is often cherished.

Learning to enjoy being alone without being lonely may take practice:

■ *Practice seeing.* You can start by enjoying the use of your senses. Look around at people and enjoy the expressions on their faces. Observe their clothing, their ways of walking and speaking. Watch pets at play. Look at the beauty of nature around you. If you're in the city, observe the architecture. Try to get outside of yourself every day by seeing one new thing in your world, something you may never have noticed before.

A computer programmer who runs every day tells me, "I only do it *partly* for exercise. The other reason is to get out. I see things as I run that I don't see from the car. When I come back from an early morning run, I feel as if I'm in touch with the world again. Sometimes I wonder what would happen if I didn't have that, at least once in a while."

■ *Practice listening.* I asked Patricia, a sales representative who owns her own house, what she liked most about living alone. Her answer sounded a little flip, but she was serious: "Playing music at full decibel."

Listening to music when you are alone is for many a great antidote to loneliness (as long as the music you choose doesn't rub salt in any wounds). If it's talk you want to hear (or virtually any other sound), your radio or TV is always there for you. All you have to do is listen.

■ *Practice touch.* As Joan said: "I brought myself satin sheets. My bed is under the window. I lie there on Sunday morning, drink my coffee, and read a book . . . with the sun shining in on my satin sheets. It feels wonderful!"

■ *Challenge your senses.* If you've had enough of high-decibel music, find silence and explore it. If your daily life is filled with advertising, TV, and high-energy images, seek out some peaceful images (a tree, a sculpture, the stars, a sunset). If you are surrounded by creature comforts every day, maybe you'll be stimulated by a stark physical challenge that will test your awareness, your endurance, or your ability to handle things in tough circumstances.

■ *Down with shoulds.* Relish what you're doing without wishing for something you can't have right now or wishing to change something that can't be changed. This could be the most difficult task of all. TV and advertising bombard us with images of the people that we "should" be, of things we "should" own, of places where we "should" be living.

These shoulds can be poisonous to your well-being. Reject them! Stop comparing your real situation with *someone else's.* It's an invalid comparison.

A Loneliness Survival Guide

Ultimately, you are your own best guide, but as you may have found, it's sometimes very difficult to find a way out when you're feeling lonely.

So instead, try being your own guide at a time when you're feeling good about yourself. In your notebook make a list of things you can do the next time you're lonely.

You may have checked off a number of social strategies (see Part One) to be part of your list. Or you may have strategies of your own that have worked for you in the past. Put them into your own Loneliness Survival Guide.

The following is a Loneliness Survival Guide that Carol wrote for herself:

SAMPLE LONELINESS SURVIVAL GUIDE

The last time you were lonely, you stayed in the apartment, and that was a mistake because as soon as you *had* to get out, you *did* get out, and you felt better. LESSON: Get out of the apartment! But first, call someone. Then get out. Last time this lonely feeling happened, you didn't want to go anywhere. This time, you're going to go someplace nice for a walk. When you do, you'll be glad you did.

If you're feeling lonely today, here's what I think you should do:

- Call around until you find someone who wants to have dinner. Make plans for this evening. *Right now!*
- Done that? Okay, now, get out of the apartment. Go see the Hendersons. They're always glad to see you. Take something for Trish. Don't stay long. Half an hour, max. That does the trick.
- Stop at the bookstore. Get a new book.
- Okay. Have a nice lunch. A really nice lunch. With your book. That'll be great.
- Go for a walk. By the river or the state park trail that's so beautiful.
- Go home, fix some tea, and read some more.
- Take a nap.
- Go to dinner.

- Now is your time to talk.
- Consider a movie.

This Loneliness Survival Guide is just a sample that worked for Carol. Tailor your own list to fit your needs. Maybe you just want names on your list—people to call. Or activities—all the things you like to do. Or specific reminders to yourself to take action.

Add to it. Think of new things. Every time you do something new—especially something that you enjoyed doing alone—put it in your Loneliness Survival Guide for future reference at a time when you may not be thinking positively.

Extending Friendships

Friends can sometimes help you cope with loneliness. But friendships can't always bear the weight of one person coming across as being too needy. On the other hand, you may fear expressing your feelings to others too much.

Ray, a thirty-five-year-old city newspaper editor, was one of the foursome that occasionally got together for poker. Kenny, the president of a heating-and-cooling operation, was the only other single member of the group. Ray and Kenny had done some whitewater rafting together, and they occasionally got together for drinks. But theirs was still, basically, a strictly masculine poker-and-beer friendship.

One night Kenny called up to cancel a poker game. Ray said, "I'm sorry it's called off. I was really looking forward to being with you guys tonight. Not so much for poker, but for the company."

Ray felt his friendship with Kenny changed after that brief conversation where they discovered they had something in common. After that, they would sometimes talk about living alone, past relationships, frustrations, and, occasionally, loneliness.

Can you take the risk of showing your feelings with someone? If so, maybe you can extend the friendship one step further.

Martha, a forty-three-year-old fashion designer, had a close friend, Lynda, who often listened to her when she was feeling lonely. Frequently, these conversations occurred when Martha was in between relationships and not dating. Martha sensed she was trying her friend's patience—but since Lynda was always easy to talk to, she continued to avail herself of Lynda's support.

One night when they were on the phone, Lynda said, "Martha, can't you ever take some responsibility for your pattern with men and how needy you feel when you're not attached?"

Martha was extremely upset by her friend's remark. It not only felt cruel to her, it seemed as if Lynda was trying to push her away. But the attitude reflected by Lynda's words slowly began to make sense to her. What if she were not really as powerless—as much of a victim—as she portrayed herself? Maybe she could learn to stop pinning so much hope on each new relationship—and then not feel so let down when it ended.

Lynda gave Martha an alternative view and it helped her.

If you turn to friends for support during those times when you are feeling lonely, consider the following strategies:

■ *Try some other levels of friendship.* If you and your friends *usually* chat about everyday things, touch upon some topics that are closer to you—a relationship, a decision you're facing, a feeling about your home or family. Try talking about someone you care about, someone you miss, or someone you admire.

■ *Ask for feedback or advice.* Listen to it, but don't feel *compelled* to follow it. Consider subjective feedback as another point of view. Learn by it how other people see things, use what applies and appreciate another's point of view, even if you don't agree with it.

■ *And, of course, reciprocate.* If you have the opportunity to help another person to gain confidence, get some new information, or make a choice that will make a difference in his or her life; be as willing to give help as you are to take it. Let your life experience be a resource for someone else who is looking for feedback and support. You can then make a good friendship stronger as your interest in that person's success becomes an additional bond.

What Can You Do When You Want Some Support?

Some suggestions:

■ *Don't be afraid to reach out!* I've given many illustrations of how people have done this successfully. Take the risk *but don't exhaust the patience of your support network.*

Listen as much as you talk. If the conversation becomes a one-way street, your friends will lose interest and eventually avoid you. Confidantes want to know that *their* issues are important, too.

Fran, a married woman in her fifties, has a good friend of the same age who calls almost nightly. "I just put the phone on the pillow and let her talk," says Fran. "Every now and then, I say, 'Uh-huh, uh-huh.' Now I'm trying to avoid her phone calls—and I feel awful about doing that. But what can I do? I am a friend to her but feel very incidental—there is no reciprocity."

Fran herself has been grappling with some difficult issues in her life, but she relies on herself and some other people. Meanwhile, this friend calls nightly, but has no idea what's on Fran's mind.

So reciprocate, find a balance, and you will keep your support system intact.

■ *Don't forget to say "Thank you."* When we've put out a brushfire in our own lives, it's sometimes easy to forget the people who helped us. Send a book with a "Thanks" on the flyleaf. A record. A French pastry. A note. There are an infinite number of ways to say "Thank you."

■ *When friends are not enough.* Friends do not always have the expertise to help you if you are feeling severely depressed and without direction. So before you exhaust some valuable friendships, or if your support system just isn't enough, consider seeking professional counseling or psychotherapy.

■ *Pros and cons of relatives.* Turning to your parents, brothers and sisters, or extended family may feel like a secure thing to do, and in many cases it's appropriate. On the other hand, people who have known you since birth are often not helpful when it comes to making transitions and choices. Parents and other close family members often have a vested interest in your decisions and are less likely to guide you in the direction you have chosen. It's not that they don't want to help, of course. On the contrary, most do. Just know your situation and whether you can still remain an adult while receiving emotional support from your family.

Chapter 18

Overcoming Loneliness and Other Negative Emotions When You're Emerging from a Relationship

It is difficult for most people to overcome loneliness completely while a love relationship is ending. Being close to someone, being in love, often involves a great deal of vulnerability. When a relationship runs its course and when it's headed toward finality, you may go through a series of transitional emotions that change swiftly and unpredictably, and can even be terrifying. It is no wonder that men and women often look back at these times as a period of not being in their "right mind."

If this has happened to you recently, or if it's happening now, you may believe that the conflicting feelings of loss, grief, anger, resentment, and yearning will last forever. When you are in the midst of it, the time of pain can seem infinite. It can be very difficult to remember that these feelings won't go on forever.

There are steps you can take that may help to speed up the process.

What can you do for yourself to reduce the pain or confusion you might be feeling so that you can let go and rebuild your life?

You can use the guidelines that follow to help you let go—feel less lonely—and to deal with the emotions that you are likely to experience when coming away from a former spouse or lover.

Unpacking Your Bags

Margaret's husband had run off with another woman eleven years before. Immediately after her husband left her, she moved into her own apartment. Margaret told me that in all the eleven years that she had lived alone, she had literally never unpacked her cartons. She believed that her husband "would be coming back any time," so she didn't see the point in moving in permanently.

Margaret actually lived in an apartment where packed cartons and boxes were stacked up in every room. She had hung a few clothes in her closet, and she had a foam-rubber mattress covered with a sheet, where she slept. The place looked as if she had moved in yesterday.

Margaret is a literal and extreme example of what's usually only a metaphor to describe someone who refuses to let go of an ended relationship and get on with life. Extreme—yes. But, in a way she is representative of what many people do. Trying to cling to the past, many refuse to give up on a relationship that is clearly over.

Margaret functioned well in most areas of her life. But she didn't want her marriage to end, so she refused to accept that it was over.

But it *was* over. Her husband was remarried to a woman many years his junior, and there was no evidence to suggest to Margaret that he was unhappy in this marriage, or that there was the slightest chance of his coming back.

After several sessions of individual counseling, Margaret entered one of my divorce groups, where she eventually told her story. The group members listened to the "unpacked bags" scenario with astonishment. One group member even began to ridicule Margaret by saying, "How can you throw your life away in that manner? You must really be nuts!"

I was about to intervene when another member beat me to it. He said, "Don't we all have something about ourselves that—looked at objectively—would make others think we're nuts? *Particularly* something regarding how we hold on to our ended marriages? We can all use help with something that seems so obvious to others."

Group members characteristically offer a great amount of candid sharing about their own hang-ups and about feelings. What was revealed in this group was in many cases just as intense for each member as it was for Margaret. They all spoke of their deep emotions, of loneliness, of anger, of guilt, the plain fear that characterized this phase of their lives and their outlook for the future. This group—and many groups like it—are testimony to the unadulterated yet normal pain that one can feel when in a state of transition.

Action Steps Toward a New Beginning

It can be very hard to admit to ourselves that we may never again be with someone we love or once loved. Or that a fixture in our lives has left, that now we are alone when we were so used to being a couple. No matter how bad the ended relationship might have been, at least it was familiar territory. It's possible we were addicted to the person *or* the lifestyle. It probably became comfortable (even if it was merely a comfort-able state of discomfort). Relinquishing that security, even though it is illusory, can be the most painful step of all.

But there are ways to let go—and to do it more quickly—before you waste any more of your valuable time.

Here is a list of "Things to Remember When Break-ing Up." Not all of these suggestions will apply to you specifically or to the relationship that has ended or is ending. But as you look at this list, you can decide what applies to your particular situation.

THINGS TO REMEMBER WHEN BREAKING UP

1. It's your responsibility to break emotionally with the other person, not the other person's responsibility to free you.

2. If it feels like you have lost your identity, real-ize that you probably deposited too much of it into the relationship in the first place.

3. Remember your ex as he or she *really* was, not in the idealized version of a person who will take care of all your needs and loneliness now.

4. Feelings of desperately needing that person do not indicate love. They merely indicate longing and need. Don't confuse these with love. You really *can* live without him or her. Trust yourself and you'll probably live even better.

5. Even if there is a lot of love between you, love is not enough to maintain a relationship. Even mu-tual love is only, at best, one important element in maintaining a relationship.

6. *Certain* things about yourself you probably won't change. Very little about the other person can be changed by you alone. That means it's possible that the relationship can't under any circumstances be worked out.

7. The feelings of sadness, anger, and pain are temporary. If you accept them, they'll pass. Then the possibilities for how you might live your life become much more open.

8. I've never met a person who truly wanted his or her ex back. More likely, you want an ideal version of your ex, without the traits that made the relationship end in the first place.

9. You can let go, if only you believe you can.

Taking Action

Right now, you may be reflecting on a love relationship that seemed unconsummated, a relationship that happened a long time ago, one that was broken off recently, or one that seems to linger on in some fragmented form.

Here are some *action steps* that I recommend to those clients who are having a difficult time with this transitional stage of their lives. Often this positive, definite action is exactly what's needed to break away from the past, and to help us live in the present.

FOUR ACTION STEPS TOWARD A NEW BEGINNING

1. Look at where you're living now. Is it where you lived with your former spouse or lover? This may be the time to make it over—transform it—put away any reminders of the past. If you have been unhappy in this place, it may be time to move if you can. It's hard to begin to discover whether you like living on your own unless the *place* where you live feels like home. (See Part Six, "Housing," page 295.)

2. Put away things that remind you of the past. Store old letters and pictures. You may not want to throw them away. You may even appreciate or cherish them some day. But for now, the best thing may be to get them out of sight.

3. Put your relationship in the present tense. Some friendships are based on griping and grievances about former lovers, old friends, or past disasters. Try to put friendships on a new footing—focusing on current plans, activities, and interests. If certain friends won't leave the painful past behind, maybe you'd be better off leaving *them* behind for a while.

4. Try to avoid thinking or saying words like "always," "never," and "forever." Such words may be loaded with dire or drastic meanings for you right now. When you find yourself asking, "Am I *always* going to feel this rotten?" "Am I *never* going to be in a relationship again?" or "Will I live alone *forever?*" recognize these questions as another expression of your panic. The answers will come, but for now accept your uncer-

tainty. Sometimes resolution comes faster if you leave things be.

Each of these steps leads toward a positive affirmation: you do not have to be tormented by your past.

Your past contains many memories—some painful and some joyous. But the past cannot be changed. Where your life is today is the only thing that can change.

If you feel tormented by the past, it could be because you would like to go back and do things again but differently. Perhaps you think the outcome would be different.

But our lives don't have rewind buttons. You can't turn back and do things over again. Accepting where you *are* is really your present task. If you can do just one thing, each day, that you would not have done if you were in the relationship, you can begin the slow, gradual healing process. Don't expect everything to fall into place overnight. And give yourself credit for each step along the way.

Chapter 19

Stopping the Emotional Pain of Breaking Up

The transition from marriage or a relationship to single life can be a time of sudden, sharp emotions. Feelings of freedom and joy can be interspersed with moments of longing and pain.

For better or worse, the relationship is over and now you're out on your own. But in the process of emotionally ending a love relationship, you may have difficulty letting go because you literally are addicted either to the person or to your former lifestyle. This addiction causes you to feel extremes of emotion after the person is gone—and all this longing adds up to some very painful feelings.

What are the words—or the messages in your head—that you may be telling yourself?

Anger:	"I could kill that person for leaving me!"
	"It's his/her fault that my life is so miserable."
Hopelessness:	"I'm trapped inside these four walls, and there's nothing I can do about it."

"No one cares about me."

"This is the end."

"I'm going to be lonely for the rest of my life."

"I'll die alone and nobody will care."

Self-blame: "If only I hadn't been so selfish and demanding, he/she wouldn't have left me and I wouldn't be alone."

Depression: "Life is so empty."

"There's nothing to look forward to."

Self-anger: "No one would want to be seen with me."

"I haven't been taking care of myself, and I look terrible."

"I am worthless."

Desperation: "I'm sad all the time. I just can't shake the loneliness and misery. And it's getting worse."

Anger, hopelessness, self-blame, depression, self-anger, and desperation are the *feelings* that often accompany loneliness. Underlying these feelings are certain beliefs about your situation, your ex, and yourself. If you look at the statements in the right-hand side of the above list, you will see that each of them in some way expresses a belief. In other words, if you *believe* it's the other person's fault for leaving you, the emotion you are likely to feel is anger. Similarly, if you *believe* you're "trapped inside these four walls" with no options, you are likely to feel hopelessness as a result of that belief.

Emotions are the result of your beliefs. Even extreme emotions such as these don't indicate that you are abnormal or weak. But if they are there, they need to be dealt with. And to achieve greater control over them, begin by looking at the underlying beliefs.

To help yourself do this, consider the following four-part strategy for mastering loneliness.

A Four-Part Strategy for Mastering Loneliness

1. *Try to look at your underlying beliefs or assumptions when you are in a rational frame of mind, not when you're upset.* For example, if you have the belief "Life is so empty," the feeling of emptiness might seem overwhelming to you. Instead, try to step back and look at that belief. For example, suppose you had a friend who was ending an inappropriate relationship: you would clearly see that your friend's life was not as empty as he or she saw it. To you, it seems clear that your friend will probably get through this and have another relationship when the time is right. You can see all the good qualities that make your friend a valuable person with a full life ahead. In fact, it might be quite clear to you that your friend is better off without the person who is the object of such longing and loneliness.

When you are in the midst of emotional pain, it is difficult to affirm to yourself that your life is *not* empty.

That is your challenge—to be a rational friend to your emotional self. And it's a difficult but possible challenge. Try—alone or with help—to make a rational observation of your irrational beliefs.

One way to help yourself is by using the "act as if . . ." technique. Challenge yourself to act as if your life were full right now. If that were the case, what would you do differently? What is it that you *can't* do now that you *could* do if you believed the affirmation that your life is full? Is it *really* true that you can't do it now? What is making you tell yourself that you *can't*?

Chances are, you can put what you need into your life through imagery.

Lloyd, a single man in his late forties, had recently lost his job and been divorced after twenty-four years of marriage. Both events occurred within six months of each other. The emotional pain was very intense—but in the midst of that, he soon made a very interesting career choice, and he established a wide circle of friends.

"I had to make up a new image of myself," he said. "No more solid-type Lloyd, the family man. Now I'm a single gentleman of wide experience and considerable leisure, with many friends to call on. At first, I just played it that way to pretend that my life was full of people and events. But now it's actually true. I *do* have a lot of places to go and people to see. That's helping the pain to wear off—and there are more times when I'm saying to myself, 'This is all right. Everything's going to be fine.'"

2. *When the feelings seem overwhelming, resist the urge to do things you'll be sorry for later.* For instance, when the loneliness seems unbearable, you might have the urge to contact your ex—whereas in the right frame of mind you wouldn't consider it.

You might be tempted to take a job opportunity *just* so you can move far away. Or you might rebound into an inappropriate new relationship just to get away from the previous one. Or perhaps you are so angry that you dwell on ways to hurt your ex, to compensate for the hurt you feel.

Don't take *anything* to extremes that has to do with your ex if you might regret it later. Instead, focus on what you can have. Explore being alone, meeting *new* people, and having new experiences. Thoughts, emotions, impulses that make you *react* to your ex are often not trustworthy. Think of the long-term effects of your actions. Think of the future—not the past.

3. *Avoid the additional pain of believing you will not survive this situation.* You will survive. Much of the relief that you will experience in the future may come about as a result of the healing nature of time. If you find yourself saying, "I'm not going to make it," turn the words around to "I *am* going to make it." You have survived before and you will again. Nothing can stop you.

4. *If you can talk about your painful emotions—when they occur and with someone who can provide empathy—the feelings will usually pass in a matter of minutes.* They won't stop permanently, of course. But if you can find some form of support during those periods when your feelings become very strong, you will probably discover that they come less and less often and with reduced intensity. Divorce-group members provide that type of support for each other exquisitely.

In many divorce groups, we set up a telephone network to help people when they need it most. When someone is feeling an intense emotion such as grief or anger, that person will call another member of the group. They talk about the emotion, and the support person may say things like "How can I help?"

The purpose is not to sympathize—because sympathy affirms that you should be in pain, and that is not helpful. Instead, we encourage empathy, so the other person can listen, talk about the emotion, and provide reassurance.

Danielle, a woman in one of the groups, had a brief and unsatisfying relationship with a man she met in a restaurant one evening. She recalled that evening as a time of intense emotions, when she was feeling particularly lonely and vulnerable. "If I'd had someone to call and talk to for just a minute," she said, "I probably would not have rushed into that relationship."

Another group member said that his moments of pain were like brief fits. "If I can talk to someone about how I'm feeling, it passes quickly," he said. "Otherwise, I'm stuck for hours with this longing that just won't go away."

Talking with someone can also help you take some steps in living from day to day and looking forward to the future. If you can tell your support person about your plans or goals, you may be able to help that process along. That person can not only support your effort, but also remind you of your goals.

Chapter 20

Design a New Attitude

When you take positive steps toward letting go emotionally, you are *designing new attitudes for yourself.*

Sandra, thirty-four, is co-owner of a catering business. She came to me when she was in the midst of a full-blown depression.

Ambitious and successful in her business, Sandra is also an accomplished athlete and musician (she plays the piano), and through her business she has many social contacts. To her friends and business associates, she appears self-assured, accomplished, and very much in control of her life.

When she moved to the city, she became part of a small group of close female friends. She and her friends would go out on dates together, and they frequently met and talked about many things they had in common. Sandra always had someone she could call.

But in the past two or three years, all Sandra's friends have married. Her social circle has changed completely. She is now the only single woman among her female friends. As her friends were married off, Sandra began to realize that she had entered the stage of her life where she, too, wanted to marry and have children.

Paul seemed exactly the right man for her. He was also a small-business owner, so he understood the demands. There was a great deal of mutual respect in their relationship, and to Sandra they seemed compatible in almost every way. Paul understood that Sandra had come to a time in her life when she wanted a husband and children. Sandra was making wedding plans, and she was very happy.

Suddenly, without warning, Paul dropped her. He met another woman, and his relationship with Sandra was history. Sandra was devastated. Everything had been going well for her—her relationship, her career, her social life—and now, suddenly, she was left feeling empty, hopeless, and unfulfilled.

When Sandra could think clearly, she remembered that this behavior was a pattern with Paul. He had once confessed to a long history of getting involved with women, then getting cold feet and rebounding into another relationship.

Realizing this about Paul, however, did not help Sandra. She still felt shattered. On Saturday nights, she would fall apart. She didn't want to be with her married friends because now she felt like a fifth wheel. Although she hardly respected Paul any more, still she yearned for his companionship.

After work, Sandra would sit at home crying, not calling any friends, not knowing what to do. There were nights when she thought of suicide. She felt as if life had passed her by. She blamed herself. She insisted that she never should have put so much emphasis on her career during her twenties. She looked back on past relationships and regretted that she had not concentrated on them more. She had let men go because they hadn't been "perfect." Now she wanted a second chance, but feared it was too late. She felt as if all her friends had grown up and left her behind.

Sandra had a lot, but none of it meant anything to her right now. None of it fulfilled her.

The Beliefs

From other things Sandra told me about herself, I knew that her attitudes and expectations had become a kind of mental design for her even at an early age. She had created an image of herself as a successful professional with an active social and athletic life, and many good friends. To complete this picture, she saw herself marrying a successful man (ideally, one just a bit more successful than she) and then beginning a family.

> Something went wrong [she told me]. I guess I just didn't meet the right man at the right time. It seems as if all my friends have somehow got ahead of me. I don't want to be living alone now! They're starting their families—and that's what I planned to do. I think Paul was my last chance to have children. Someone else may come along, but that could be years from now—and by then it may be too late. I've really messed up my life.

The belief was: "Since I don't have an ideal man, I can't get married and have children right now. Therefore, my whole life is ultimately meaningless."

But Sandra began to recognize that if she wanted to feel better, she had to redesign that attitude. She *could* become the designer of a new attitude—or she could be stuck with the devastating feelings that now had her in a corner. Because things hadn't worked out exactly as she expected, it would serve her well to readjust her thinking so she *would not* feel so cornered.

I asked Sandra to take that first step toward mastering her loneliness: I asked her to identify some of the assumptions that were built into her present attitude. Then we could work on some ways for her to *redesign* those assumptions—on a trial basis—so she could experience how a *new* attitude could fit her.

What if she saw her problems not as *she* saw them, but as someone *else* might view them? What if she took the position of someone who *did* have control over her choices? Together, we looked at the alternatives.

Here are some of the issues that came up:

A G E

Sandra's Old Attitude: "I'm thirty-four years old and it's getting too late to marry anyone but the leftovers."

Alternative Attitude: "I am too young to disqualify myself from marriage. True, an appropriate partner has not yet appeared, but that doesn't mean I have to change my goals—only my time frame. I still have several years left to bear children."

FRIENDSHIPS

Sandra's Old Attitude: "Now that my friends are married, I'm just a fifth wheel. They invite me to come along only because they feel sorry for me."

Alternative Attitude: "My friends are still my friends, even though they're caught up in married life. I'm not going to give up those friendships just because their lifestyles have changed. On the other hand, I'm not obliged to always attend social functions where only couples are present. I have a choice."

RELATIONSHIPS

Sandra's Old Attitude: "I'm a loser if I don't have a promising relationship with a man."

Alternative Attitude: "My worth as a person is *not* determined by the presence or absence of a relationship. I know that it's worse to be trapped in a *bad* relationship than to be alone. Being without a man, right now, is not a catastrophe."

SELF-BLAME

Sandra's Old Attitude: "It was my fault that Paul left me. I concentrated too much on my career and not enough on pleasing him."

Alternative Attitude: "I think my relationship with Paul was probably an illusion. He was not what he appeared to be. Had this been a viable relationship in the first place, we probably would have worked things out. He just was not an appropriate partner for me, and there was nothing I could have done to change that."

LIVING ALONE

Sandra's Old Attitude: "I've blown my last chance. Now I'll be living alone for the rest of my life, and that makes life not worth living."

Alternative Attitude: "If I think of Paul as my 'last chance,' it will probably become a self-fulfilling prophecy. I'm determined to turn this experience around so that it will benefit me. I intend to meet more men and to use my past as a positive learning experience, instead of as proof that I am unworthy."

FINDING A HUSBAND

Sandra's Old Attitude: "Mere friendships with men are a waste of time. I have to find a husband."

Alternative Attitude: "I'm not going to categorize men as being potential husband candidates *or* as having no worth at all. At this time of my life, I can still spend time with men who feel no urgency at all about making commitments. On the other hand, I'm not going to seek male companionship out of desperation or because I have ulterior motives. When I *want* a lot of time to myself, I'm going to take it."

GETTING BURNED AGAIN

Sandra's Old Attitude: "Every man is going to act like Paul."

Alternative Attitude: "I've met any number of men who *do* show more loyalty than Paul, so I know they exist. In reality, I'm much better off without Paul. Sure, what he did hurt me, but I would have been much more hurt if he had not bowed out as early in the game as he did. I'm glad our lives didn't get any more entangled."

FEELING TRAPPED

Sandra's Old Attitude: "I'm going to be stuck exactly where I am for the rest of my life."

Alternative Attitude: "Who can predict? I think it's likely that I'm going to have many more chances. I

> am not going to add to my
> pain by assuming that this
> situation is permanent."

If any of Sandra's old attitudes sound familiar to you, consider some of the alternative attitudes that could help change the negatives to positives. You can design your own attitudes about your life—and you can do it consciously rather than just accepting the values that society or your upbringing have mandated.

The moment that you begin to design your own attitudes, you will take greater control of your life. Instead of blaming circumstances and individuals who let you down, you can exercise your power to shape something new out of your life.

Three Wise Friends

As a next step to mastering her loneliness, Sandra had to avoid some of the emotional impulses that she might regret later. Several times, she tried to reach Paul, and when she got through, his coldness only increased her pain. She was considering selling her part of the business and moving out of the city—though she had no idea where she would like to go or what she wanted to do.

I suggested to Sandra that the next time she had a sudden impulse to do something she might later regret, she should consult "three wise friends." In other words, if she had to pick three wise friends and let them counsel her, what would they say?

In Sandra's case, those three wise friends might say things like:

> Sandra is feeling particularly hopeless right now because Paul let her down so hard. But we know

that the way he behaved really has little to do with her. As soon as she wants, she can be with people who enjoy her company—and in all likelihood, she will have the kind of relationship she would like to have. If she could just look around the corner, a few months from now, she would see that this is all going to be over soon and she would feel much better.

If you can think of "three wise friends"—a composite of the three wisest people you know— and imagine their conversation in your head, you'll probably discover that their views are much more well-considered and reasonable than your own.

For instance, if you say, "I want to sell everything, quit my job, and move out of town," they will probably reply:

> Of course you do. You are surrounded by reminders of the person you are missing. But even if you leave town tomorrow, the reminders will follow you wherever you go—and the negative feelings that you are experiencing without that person will be just as powerful. Perhaps the best prescription for you is time and patience to let the wounds heal. Then see what you want to do.

You *can* give advice to yourself—and good advice, at that. If you put yourself in a meeting with these three people, you will be impressed with their sound advice. Those wise friends represent your hidden wisdom, which will emerge if you let them speak.

For example, you might be saying to yourself, "I want to get back at my ex."

But your three wise friends would caution:

> Getting back at your ex won't *bring* that person back into your life. In fact, if you do that, you're likely to inflict more pain on yourself by demon-

strating that your ex no longer cares about you. The best action may be to get on with your *own* life—living your own life well is probably the best revenge.

Of course, this is your own sound reasoning coming through your three friends. But you *do* know what they will probably say, and you would probably give them similar advice. So why don't you use some of your own counseling skills with yourself?

Desperation

Sandra also had to deal with her desperation, the thought that she wouldn't survive, she wouldn't make it. The worst part about this was the sense of helplessness that overcame her at times. She would be sitting at home thinking everything she did was wrong, every action a mistake; every feeling drove her more deeply into pain and depression. How could she take that crucial next step? How could she convince herself that she *would* survive, that this wound *would* heal?

For Sandra, making her own Loneliness Survival Guide (like that on page 108) was extremely helpful in getting her through these times. First on her list, in the Survival Guide, was "Practice the piano." Second came "Tennis"—and she had a list of tennis partners with their phone numbers. She also had suggestions to herself for the rest of the day and evening. But by the time she finished up at the tennis club, she was already beginning to make plans. It was just a matter of taking those first one or two steps—to get *moving* again—that made all the difference.

Finding Empathy

In the first few weeks after she broke up with Paul, Sandra sometimes felt as if she were hiding behind a wall of shame. The relationship had been "so exciting, so perfect," that she had rushed along for months in a "swirl of happiness." All her friends knew about Paul. They knew Sandra wanted to marry him.

Then she was "dumped." She could not think of any other word for it. She wanted to "bury her head, hide in the sand, never see anyone again, never *talk* to anyone again."

She needed some support. She longed to talk to her friends. But she was hiding instead.

Sandra had to take the fourth step toward breaking away—to find support to help the worst of the feelings pass. But she was also fighting with her own image of herself, the image of a successful, energetic woman in control of her life. Many of her friendships were established through business contacts, when she had been in an extremely different frame of mind. She didn't know whether she could take those friendships to a next level. She didn't know *how to reach out without feeling helpless.*

To help Sandra, I suggested she try calling someone with whom she had shared a good experience. The previous summer, Sandra had gone sailing with Amy, a business colleague. Sandra had not previously confided in Amy about the breakup with Paul, but still she thought Amy was someone who might understand and perhaps listen.

When she called Amy at home, Sandra simply began by asking, "Amy, do you remember that day we went sailing last summer? I had a great time. I wondered if you'd like to plan another one."

They made plans. Before the conversation was over,

Amy asked, "Sandra, how's it going? I was sorry to hear that you broke up with Paul."

"I'm miserable," Sandra replied bluntly.

That broke the ice! They talked for an hour, and found out that they had much more in common than they had realized. There is nothing magic here—just the idea that supportive friends are out there if only you seek them and take the first step.

The Gift of Time

When a relationship has ended, you may suddenly find that you have a lot of extra time on your hands. Filling those once busy hours can seem like a great burden.

If you and your ex shared in social activities, recreation, and time at home, this found time can seem like your worst enemy. In the absence of your usual activities—as well as your usual companion—the loneliness often seems harsh.

Andrew recalled the panic he felt when he faced this sudden abundance of time. He had recently left his wife with whom he had lived for several years:

> I always used to do things for other people— things I was expected to do. And whenever my wife and I made plans together, we were usually planning for both of us, not just for me alone. I'm just beginning to realize I've never had to *deal* with having a huge amount of free time all to myself. It left a void in my life.

For Andrew, the solution was in doing things that had primarily been handled by his wife. He began calling friends, writing letters, making plans. He decided that it was important to get away for an adventurous vacation. Within a month of his separation, he had planned a rafting trip on the Colorado River with some friends from the West Coast. (The idea came from a photograph in an outdoor sports magazine.) He found that he had to take the initiative with his social life.

Andrew began to see how much he had feared what might happen to him after the relationship ended. Although the relationship had not been wholly satisfying, it had fulfilled certain needs, and being in that relationship had distracted him from taking new risks. Once he realized he was able to take some risks and try some new things, it wasn't so difficult for Andrew to get moving again in his life.

He was able to fill the void that he had felt initially when the relationship ended. And he saw how ludicrous it was to hold on to a relationship just because he feared that emptiness in his life.

In fact, many people do stay in relationships that aren't working, primarily because they fear the issue of how they'd fill all that time by themselves. If you're worried about all the hours that stretch ahead unfilled, it's helpful to think about that free time as a gift that is yours to use *creatively* to expand your own interests and, in doing so, to enlarge your circle of friends.

Rough Times Now and Then

The most important thing to realize when you're in a tough situation is that it's not forever. If you think back to the rough spots you've experienced before, you may gain some perspective on this important idea. To make this kind of retrospection a positive exercise, try the following:

Think back to some of the times in your life when you hit bottom or came close—when you lost your job, when other relationships ended, when you lost a loved one through death, or when some well-thought-out plan simply did not work.

Then remember how, one way or another, you came up out of the ashes.

What was the process that helped you do this? Perhaps you made the job, or the experience, or the person less important in your life. Perhaps it was *time* that helped you heal. Perhaps it was talking over the situation with other people who cared about you. Perhaps it was self-pride in learning that you had the strength to handle it and the wisdom to look at a bad experience *not* as a problem but as a *challenge* to your ingenuity and courage.

If you can think this way about what's happening, you will see that you are already in the process of weathering the storm. The emotional turmoil that has been almost an obsession or a constant stream is becoming less and less severe.

The change is gradual at first, which may fool you into thinking that your pain is just as intense as it was before. But loneliness and other negative emotions do begin to come less frequently, to lessen dramatically, or to stop completely. And, finally, at a certain point we can begin to characterize ourselves as something other than a person in transition. We are not becoming—*we have become!*

Part Three

Romantic Strategies

The art of living single also means knowing when you want to move toward a relationship.

Are You Looking for Commitment?

If you do want a relationship, how do you start the process of finding an appropriate partner?

If you *really* want a relationship, how much energy are you willing to put into the search?

Do the benefits of living single outweigh the benefits of becoming involved—or even living with another person?

Do you believe you *should* be in a relationship? And, if so, is that your own voice telling you that you should—or is it the voice of your parents, friends, or "society"?

In this section, you will have the opportunity to answer such questions for yourself. I encourage you to complete the Attitude Inventories that are included in this chapter and to read the evaluation that accompanies each Inventory. Among the issues these inventories are meant to clarify:

- Do you *want* involvement? (page 150)
- If you say you want a relationship, but you don't have one, do you think there's something wrong with you? (Page 159)
- What is an *inappropriate* partner? (page 177)
- What happens when you decide the goal *is* involvement? (page 209)
- How can you nurture a relationship? (page 222)
- How can you manage relationships and still be a good single parent? (page 230)
- The perils of sex—what do they mean to you? (page 241)

Chapter 21

Enjoying Single Life

You have the power to decide what you want and to find the path that will make that decision a reality.

VANESSA

For the single person ending a relationship, the *chance* to be single can be an opportunity in self-discovery. Vanessa, twenty-nine, had several male companions before she and Eric moved in together. Their relationship ended after three years.

When I met Eric, I had only been alone a few days. I'd never had time to be by myself and remember the things I like to do and reestablish a relationship with myself. I've taken this time to remember and rediscover what I like to do.

The relationship ended last summer. I'm still carrying baggage from it, but it's over. After I broke up with him, I thought what I would miss most was being with someone who was so incredibly bright. I thought, Gee, that's over, he was just *so* intelligent, and now I won't have that stimulation. Then it occurred to me: Wait a minute, why can't I do that for myself? So I took on self-evaluation as a project. I even forced myself to read things that, normally, I would never have read.

I realized I wasn't used to being on my own. I had always had a boyfriend—for *years* I had a boyfriend. If I broke up with someone, I'd meet someone else almost the next day. So this period of being on my own is very good. Now I accept and understand the fact that the development of a relationship has its own timing. This is a time to get to know myself better.

I now *choose* to do things on my own, on purpose. I actually made a list of things I wanted to do alone. I could have gone out with a friend on Saturday night, but I didn't. I wanted to go by myself. I now want to find out what it's like to be *me*—on my own.

Obviously a relationship is a possibility in the future, but for Vanessa, the challenge (now that she's between relationships) is to use her time alone to explore and rediscover for herself all the things she likes to do.

SEAN

A forty-three-year-old lawyer who was divorced four years ago, Sean is looking for ways to meet women. But he does not want a relationship to rush toward commitment.

I've met people mostly through introductions by mutual friends. For me, those usually turn out to be the best relationships. Somehow, having a proper introduction is different from meeting someone in the art museum, or sitting in a subway, or in a club. Mutual friends are most likely to select people who are more *like* you, as opposed to people you may meet randomly in more informal settings.

The city I live in also has a good singles network. At parties for single men and women I've hit it off with a couple of really nice women. I'm also good at meeting people at a formally organized party.

Although he expects to remarry at some point, Sean finds that many women have expectations that he is not prepared to meet early in a relationship.

I find that I'm having to work harder than I used to, to control the expectations of a woman when we first get together. I make sure I'm not leading her on. Or—if we go out more than once in a week—that it is not necessarily something exclusive.

I'm not possessive with women, and I don't make many demands on them. I don't like to manipulate them into doing what they don't want to do. But I do expect them to reciprocate, and to give me the space and freedom that I'm more than happy to give them.

For me, the best part of relationships is starting them. That's where there's the real fire, the interest, and the curiosity. It seems like, after several months, some of that fire and interest evaporates. But I thrive on *beginning* relationships. That's the really sensational part of being single.

At this time, Sean does not want to give up the advantages of being single in favor of a committed relationship, though he remains open to the possibility.

JOAN

A thirty-seven-year-old design consultant, Joan has joint custody of her eight-year-old child.

> Having a child adds some difficulty to the *dating* part of my being single. It is definitely an issue that comes up in every relationship that I'm in. Either men don't have children—and would like to—and wonder whether I'd still be interested, or they have children of their own and think about blending families, either pro or con.

> And *time* is a factor. Because my son is only with me half the time, I am not really that keen on getting baby-sitters when he is with me. When he's *not* with me, I travel a lot on business. So I have a much more limited amount of time to date than other single people who don't have children, or whose children are grown.

Joan considers herself idealistic about the man she would like to meet. She often finds that the men to whom she is most attracted are those who enjoy being single.

> In many respects, the kind of people I enjoy being with—though they may not be relationship-oriented—are the ones who are satisfied with the way things are now.

When she weighs the advantages of being single against the advantages of being in a relationship, Joan finds that she has to become comfortable with a certain predictable amount of insecurity.

> I think the worst thing about being single is juggling a variety of commitments and trying to build relationships before you have a real sense of how they're going to turn out. So I have to keep

one foot into maintaining a variety of friendships and in dating, while at the same time trying to find and build a long-term relationship. It's not so much that either one of those things is unpleasant—it's the *sitting on the fence* part of it, of never having a sense of permanency or a feeling of security, and being okay about that.

Although life is unpredictable whether you're married or single, at least when you're married there's the *intention* of sharing your future with somebody else. There's a game plan, and you can believe in the game plan, whether it ultimately turns out the way you want it or not.

I miss that. To tell the truth, I do.

MARLA

The executive administrator for a nonprofit organization, listed in *Who's Who Among American Women,* Marla was divorced when she was twenty-nine. "It took me about two years to get over it," she observes. During that time she was dating with "no serious intention," while putting more time and energy into her professional development. Now thirty-four, she is living "quite comfortably" single. She says her greatest difficulty is meeting "quality people."

My dilemma is to meet a professional man who is well educated, and who does the same things that I do—namely, spends time working and being with friends, and who is not hanging out in singles bars.

I don't go out dancing or drinking. I don't join singles clubs, I don't join film clubs or whatever else is out there. I am a busy professional.

Also, I'm a homeowner, so I need a certain

amount of weekend time to maintain my home. I tend to go to gatherings with a fairly small circle of good friends. I enjoy it quite a bit, but that lifestyle does not allow me to see enough new faces.

As a female professional who's somewhat high-powered, I guess part of my concern is having a relationship in which I could preserve at least most—if not necessarily all—of my identity. I wonder how I would integrate my occasional lack of availability and my devotion to outside things into an ongoing relationship. My concern is that I will want to preserve too many parts of my current lifestyle in any future lifestyle.

Marla's standards for a partner are high. Because of her lifestyle, she sees her social contacts as being limited and likely to remain so. At the present time, she is unwilling to consider lowering her standards or changing her lifestyle significantly in order to begin a relationship. She has answered a few personal ads and says: "It's an interesting experience. I've met several people. Nothing has gone very far. But I find, given my time constraints and how I spend my time, personal ads are an efficient way of meeting people who are interested in meeting *other* people."

Looking at Involvement

Vanessa, Sean, Joan, and Marla have each made certain choices for themselves, based upon past relationships and upon current commitments to career, family, friends, and lifestyle. For Vanessa the end of a long-term relationship was an opportunity to understand herself better, to develop her own interests, and to explore the possibilities of being alone. Right now, remaining single has a greater attraction for her than finding another relationship.

Although he says he is looking for a relationship that might lead to commitment, Sean acknowledges that for him the best part of a relationship comes with the initial interest and excitement. Since his divorce, he has avoided both a long-term commitment and a monogamous relationship. But he wants to meet new women and continue relationships in which there is ample freedom on both sides.

Joan finds herself doing a balancing act. She wants to spend time with her child, continue the career that she finds satisfying, and maintain friendships, but also leave herself open to the possibility of a relationship. At the same time, she is strongly attracted to some of the positive aspects of married life, and there are times when that is clearly what she wants.

Marla wants a relationship, but only with someone who is in every way her equal. And that person must permit her to continue the lifestyle that she values very highly. At the same time, she recognizes that many of her social contacts are with people she already knows. That, together with her high standards for a prospective partner, limits her range of choices.

What choices are you considering? How important to you is finding a relationship—and what are the factors that you have to consider *before* making a commitment? How much are you willing to change your lifestyle, your priorities, or your criteria in order to get what you want?

Do you really want involvement?

Chapter 22

Do You Want Involvement?

In part, the decision whether or not to have a relationship is a *lifestyle choice*. So to help you to clarify some choices about your lifestyle, refer to the Attitude Inventory below. Think about whether you would respond YES or NO to each statement, and write your answers in a notebook. Then refer to the Evaluation at the end of this inventory as a personal guide.

ATTITUDE INVENTORY I
Living Alone/Seeking a Relationship

	YES	NO	
1.	(Y)	(N)	I would be ready to relocate if it would increase my chances of having a relationship.
2.	(Y)	(N)	I would be willing to make serious changes in my career plans or professional goals to improve my chances of finding a romantic partner.

3. (Y)   (N)   I would be willing to make signifi-
                cant changes in my schedule to ac-
                commodate the needs of a potential
                partner.

4. (Y)   (N)   I would adjust my living habits and
                negotiate matters of personal taste
                in order to share living arrange-
                ments with a significant other.

EVALUATION—ATTITUDE INVENTORY I

Answering YES to these questions is an indication
that you are more willing to compromise to move toward a relationship. To take this evaluation a step
further, it will be helpful also to look at your NO answers. For each NO answer, ask yourself if there are
certain conditions under which you would change a NO
to a YES. Be honest with yourself, because you could
be staring right at your strongest conflict about getting
what you want.

If most of your answers to this evaluation are NO,
meeting a potential partner is not as much of a priority
as you think. So your task is to consider changing that
attitude, or to concentrate on enhancing and enjoying
life as a single.

Lifestyle Changes

During one of my radio call-in programs, where we
were discussing singles lifestyles, a caller who identified himself as Andrew raised the following point:

I live in a small town and I go to work just a few miles away. Apart from that, I don't travel much. So when you talk about meeting new people, seeing new faces, that doesn't mean much to me. I've known just about all the women around here since I was a kid, and I've dated everyone I'm interested in. Sure, I'd like to get married and settled down, but I don't have many chances to meet new partners.

As we discussed some alternatives, it became apparent that Andrew didn't want to make any major changes in his lifestyle. He was comfortable where he was living, and he enjoyed the circle of friends that he'd grown up with. I pointed out that he *was* making a choice by holding on to his lifestyle. He obviously did not want to change or risk that lifestyle.

Like Andrew, you may be living in an area where there seem to be very few potential mates, and your life does not include a *plan* for escaping from the parameters of the place you're living in.

Andrew, for instance, could have considered moving to a new and larger community, even a big city, if his desire to meet a new and wider group of single females outweighed, on balance, his desire to remain in a town that was familiar to him.

I suggested to Andrew that he look into a national organization that would afford him opportunities to travel. Compared to a change in lifestyle, traveling does not require such a major commitment.

Among the categories of such organizations:

- A sports organization or club that would be likely to have single female as well as male members
- Business or professional associations
- A group dealing with a particular hobby or interest

- A charitable or nonprofit organization
- A club with an educational or cultural affiliation

In Andrew's case, either relocating or joining a group such as those above could significantly increase the probability that he will meet an appropriate partner.

If your Attitude Inventory I shows that you *are* willing to make some lifestyle changes, you obviously will increase your chances of finding the relationship you want.

ATTITUDE INVENTORY II
Personal Criteria:

Whom Would You Consider as a Potential Partner?

Respond to this inventory by numbering 1 through 11 in your notebook. Then write TRUE or FALSE beside each number. The evaluation at the end of this inventory will help you interpret your responses.

	TRUE	FALSE	
1.	T	F	I do not want as a potential partner someone who does not meet my criteria physically (overweight, too short, etc.).
2.	T	F	I want to avoid certain habits such as smoking, overeating, or sloppiness.
3.	T	F	I would never go out with a person who was involved with someone else.

4. T F I prefer a partner within a certain age group (same age, older, or younger).

5. T F I would like the person to have achieved certain educational levels (high school, college grad, graduate school).

6. T F I would like a partner who is making a certain amount of money.

7. T F I would avoid a relationship with someone who has children.

8. T F I would not consider someone who wants (or doesn't want) children.

9. T F I would avoid an interracial or interfaith relationship.

10. T F I would avoid someone who asked me to give up or restrict my career, even temporarily.

11. T F I would not want a recently divorced or separated person.

EVALUATION—ATTITUDE INVENTORY II

Each TRUE in your response column indicates that you have a criterion that in some way limits your field of choice. Use your responses as statements of insight and decide how flexible or inflexible you are willing to be.

What Are Your Personal Criteria?

We all have certain criteria that we apply to other people and to ourselves. Marla, as you recall, has a strong self-image as a highly successful, highly motivated individual. Thus, she applies very strict criteria regarding men whom she would consider as acceptable partners. But Marla has found a way both to maintain her standards and to find more men who meet those standards.

She is aware that, in setting these criteria, she *has* limited her range of choice. On the other hand, she also places personal ads as a way of finding more men who might be interested in her—thereby *increasing* her range of choice.

What Is *Your* Control?

The power to exercise your vast personal freedom— and to explore the options available to you—depends to some degree on your ability to free yourself from preconceptions (often not really your own) about what you *should* or *ought* to be doing.

The eminent psychologist and author Dr. Albert Ellis, originator of Rational Emotive Therapy, describes these "absolutistic *shoulds*" in the following way:

> Absolutistic *shoulds* can get you into real emotional difficulty. Suppose you say to yourself, for example, "I *should* marry in order to be happy." What you mean is not only that it may be preferable for you to marry and that you will in all probability be happier married than unmarried, but you may also mean, "No matter what, I *must* get married. If I don't marry, I can't be happy at

all! What is more, if I don't marry it will probably be because I am a crummy person who isn't able to marry anybody decent. And that is *terrible!*" If this is what you mean by your *should,* you are really in trouble!

When, in other words, your *shoulds* and *oughts* are unconditional and absolutistic, you are really saying that *under all conditions,* you *should* do this or not do that; that the world will practically come to an end if you don't do what you supposedly *should;* that you will then be able to have no joy whatever in life and may even die; and that your inability to carry out what you absolutely *should* makes you a thoroughly rotten, worthless individual. This kind of unconditional *should* is really a thoroughgoing, 100 percent *must,* or a *got to, have to, need to. . .*[1]

Dr. Ellis's statement is hard-hitting, but true. How does it apply to you?

Practical and Emotional Solutions

There are at least two kinds of solutions to every problem. One is changing the circumstances outside of yourself. The second, as emphasized by Albert Ellis, is an emotional solution—and that is to change the way you *look* at the problem and at yourself *as a result.*

If what you want is to find a relationship, then if and when you find one you have achieved a *practical* solution. In the meantime, until you find that relationship, you can still work on and achieve an *emotional* solution. This is self-acceptance. Self-acceptance is not contingent on whether you are in a relationship. It is

1. Albert Ellis and Irving M. Becker, *A Guide to Personal Happiness* (North Hollywood: Wilshire Book Company, 1982).

your ability to accept circumstances and to accept yourself. The good news about the emotional solution is that once you have it, *nobody* can take it away. Relationships don't have that safeguard.

On the other hand, if you have determined that a relationship is not in the cards for you right now, you can work very hard on forming an attitude that allows having a relationship to be less and less important to you. Many of the strategies that I suggest throughout this book will help you acquire that attitude.

Of course, you never want to delude yourself into the false belief that you *don't* want something that you *do* want, or vice versa. But your emotional priorities can change—and you can stand by the choices that you've made for yourself or change them at any time.

Here is a simple emotional solution to being without a relationship. Change—

"I can't be happy *without* a relationship"
to
"I probably would be happi*er* with one,
but I can *still* be happy without it."

What happens when you change your attitude in this way?

For starters, you will relieve yourself of a great deal of unhappiness!

Often, the essence of unhappiness is simply feeling as though you're a victim, that you have landed in a certain set of circumstances against your will and that you have no choice, no options at all. The state of victimhood is one that we often relegate to *ourselves*— just realizing that fact can make a big difference.

Remember, relationships are only one part of your life. You can guide yourself either toward making that relationship a reality *or* toward giving yourself the acceptance you deserve whether you are in a relationship or not. So if you have determined that involvement is *not* in the cards right now, why not concentrate on your own self-acceptance?

If you are in a position where you can never quite figure out whether you want a relationship or not, that means there's a constant struggle going on inside you. Often that struggle is not pleasant. It's almost like a bad dream—reaching out for something that's always just beyond reach. And when you find yourself empty-handed, you may be asking, "What's wrong? Is it *me*? Should I be reaching farther—or are there no good ones left?"

Giving up the struggle means that you make a *choice*. You say, "I'm going to accept myself the way I am—and stop making my self-acceptance depend on something I don't have."

When you do that—what a relief!

"I'm fine just as I am!" These are the words that express a new attitude. And that attitude can be the first step toward changing your life!

Chapter 23

If You Say You Want a Relationship but Don't Have One, Do You Wonder What's Wrong with You?

You may *say* you want a relationship, and perhaps the thought of being in a loving, romantic involvement preoccupies you. But somehow you don't seem to be able to get the kind of involvement you want.

If your tendency is to start blaming people, circumstances, or yourself, you may be tempted to look upon finding a relationship as futile. For example—

- (Blaming the other sex): "There are no good ones left!"
- (Putting yourself down): "I'm unattractive, unintelligent: who would want a relationship with me?"
- (Blaming age differences in the population): "They're all so old!" or "All the good ones are older!"

But instead of giving up on the type of relationship you desire, take a few minutes to ask yourself—

- What does a potential partner need to do in order to become close to *me?*
- Do I subject my potential partners to an excessive amount of scrutiny?
- Do I emphasize traits or characteristics that are *lacking* in the people I meet rather than what's *present* in them?
- Do I make it a habit to compare prospective partners with past lovers?
- And if so, are my past lovers people whom I look upon as being *all* good or *all* bad?
- Even before the relationship begins, am I building walls to protect myself from an involvement/ lifestyle that I may not really even want?

All these are ways in which you create *emotional obstacles* that could be blocking you from involvement with the person whom you say you want in your life.

Obstacles—even emotional obstacles—are not immovable. You can get around them if that is what you want to do. Once you recognize an emotional obstacle, you can take action to change that attitude and effect more open communication with the person with whom you're becoming involved, or to seek counseling that enables you to look at your life choices and decide and implement those that are most attractive to you.

Some of these emotional obstacles we can identify and name. In the following cases, for instance, both Bill and Eileen are examples of people who are struggling with relationships and the obstacles that block them. In order to make some choices about their relationships, each of them had to recognize how their obstacles were affecting their feelings and their behavior.

BILL

The forty-two-year-old manager of a radio station, Bill has many attributes that could make a desirable partner. Bill loves his work and he is very successful. He has a beautifully furnished town house in an exclusive section of the city, and he is constantly being invited to parties, which he usually attends with personalities in radio, music, and show business.

In counseling, he said he was not being successful in finding the woman with whom he wanted to share his life, and he wanted to explore some issues around developing a relationship.

When I asked him to describe the woman he was looking for, he said she was an intelligent professional, somewhat younger, who wanted to continue to pursue her career while he pursued his. While he was not specifically interested in becoming a father, Bill said he wasn't opposed to having a child, "if that's really what she wants."

Actually, Bill had quite a long list of women he was seeing who approximately fit his description—but he said he was not getting deeply involved with any of them.

Why?

I asked Bill to list some things he would be willing to sacrifice for the sake of his relationship. He mentioned two. He said he would be willing to lighten up "somewhat" on his hours of work. And secondly, he said he would be willing to eat at home more often. To him these seemed like big changes in his lifestyle—and he said he would be willing to make those changes if the right person came along. But, he said, that woman had not come along yet:

> When it comes right down to it, practically every woman I have gone out with has wanted to

change my life. That always bothers me. I don't want to change my lifestyle very much. I'm happy with things the way they are.

The Emotional Obstacle

Bill's chief emotional obstacle was the *fear of loss of freedom*. He had decided that he was willing to make limited changes in his lifestyle if the right person came along. However, he put certain nonnegotiable limitations on the changes that he was willing to make. He enjoyed his freedom, and feared that another person entering his life might take some of that freedom away from him.

Among Bill's Choices . . .

Bill has numerous choices he can make. Without changing his lifestyle, he can continue to meet women and date frequently—but with a somewhat clearer understanding of his own unwillingness to make sacrifices for the sake of a relationship. However, he might also choose to alter his expectations of the type of woman who would accept the lifestyle he has chosen, and begin seeking a partner who is likely to place fewer demands on him. He also has the option of extending the list of changes he is willing to make in his own lifestyle for the sake of involvement.

EILEEN

I don't fall halfway in love. If a man doesn't make me feel totally, passionately attracted to him, I know it's not the real thing, and I'm not interested. I want to be swept off my feet. *That's* when I'm really happiest.

Eileen's description of romance might sound perfect to some people. There is just one thing wrong. Once she was involved with a man who "swept her off her feet," she became terrified that she would be consumed by the relationship. She feared *loss of control.*

In the cycle she was going through, she was keenly attracted to men who lavished all kinds of attention on her. She responded by giving totally, keying her feelings to the blissful moments of their romance. But when that high-level intensity began to pass, she hated and feared the feeling of being totally vulnerable and helpless. In the afterglow of her infatuation she often felt ignored, rejected, or used.

The Emotional Obstacle

The *fear of loss of control* was an emotional obstacle in Eileen's relationships. On the other hand, when she met a man who did *not* arouse an intense level of attraction, she usually concluded that the relationship was not worth pursuing. Romance, to her, meant all or nothing. But at the same time, she feared being out of control, so she would often withdraw before she could get hurt.

Among Eileen's Choices . . .

Eileen has a highly romanticized sense of what it means to be in a relationship. On the one hand, no one is good enough unless he "sweeps her off her feet"— but if he's going to sweep her off her feet, then that person becomes too frightening. Double bind!

Eileen could come to grips with the fact that she ultimately is in charge of her response—and the idea of losing control is something she can choose *not* to allow to happen. She also has the option of consciously seeking out men who don't arouse in her too high a level of intense emotion, then exercising somewhat more patience—taking more time—to see whether she can find rewards in a relationship that develops more gradually. If infatuation is what she is seeking, she might find greater enjoyment in short-term, high-intensity relationships, by recognizing that those relationships are based merely upon infatuation and a romanticized image of what it means to fall in love, and that they probably won't last.

Do You Have an Obstacle Course?

If you are facing similar circumstances in your own life—if you are finding that involvements do not last even when you want them to—it may be worthwhile to identify your own emotional obstacle course.

A Psychological Mirror

To help you find out what your emotional obstacles might be, hold up a "psychological mirror" to yourself. Find out how you appear to others. An appropriate time for this is when you're not upset or distressed, but in a relatively calm mood. If you're objective, you may be surprised at how much you can discover by looking at yourself in that psychological mirror.

To help you see your reflection in that mirror, here is a Personal Profile checklist. In your notebook, set up two columns labeled "Describes Me" and "Does Not Describe Me," and lines numbered 1 through 18. As you read through the statements below, check off each number in the "Describes Me" or "Does Not Describe Me" columns in your notebook.

PERSONAL PROFILE

	Describes Me	Does Not Describe Me	
1.	_____	_____	When I begin to reveal more about myself, I often become afraid that the other person will reject me.
2.	_____	_____	If things get too intimate and intense, I feel as though I've lost control of the ability to direct my life.
3.	_____	_____	I become too attached to the other person, and then begin to find the prospect of temporary or permanent separation too painful.
4.	_____	_____	The degree to which I fall in love is something over which I have no control.
5.	_____	_____	When I really begin to adore someone, I panic and start having serious doubts about getting more deeply involved.
6.	_____	_____	When someone is really very interested in me, I assume there must be something wrong with that person.

	Describes Me	Does Not Describe Me	
7.	____	____	If I get into a relationship, I fear that I will lose my privacy or will have to give up parts of my single lifestyle that I enjoy.
8.	____	____	If I show my commitment to the other person, the relationship is likely to take a turn for the worse.
9.	____	____	Everyone I get involved with seems to have something wrong with him (or her).
10.	____	____	Whether or not I want to, I often suffer by comparing my current partner with one I had in a previous relationship.
11.	____	____	I am afraid of someone finding out everything there is to know about me.
12.	____	____	As soon as I get to know someone better, I start to lose interest in the relationship.
13.	____	____	I always act less interested than I actually am, so the other person cannot take advantage of me.

	Describes Me	Does Not Describe Me	
14.	——	——	When a relationship turns sexual, I often wonder whether I'm being too aggressive—or not responsive enough.
15.	——	——	I'm afraid of my own ambivalence.
16.	——	——	I often seem to meet people who have some of the things I'm looking for in a partner—but not everything.
17.	——	——	I often get interested in a person who is involved in another relationship.
18.	——	——	Even when I have strong positive feelings about a relationship at first, I eventually find myself saying or doing things specifically to test the other person.

EVALUATING YOUR
PERSONAL PROFILE

This Personal Profile can help you to find some of
the emotional obstacles that may be getting in your
way when you want to become involved in a relationship. By recognizing and looking at them objectively, you may come to a better understanding of your
obstacles and how you can get past them.

Below, look for the numbers that you checked off in
the "Describes Me" column. The brief evaluation that
follows each sentence may help you understand the
obstacle(s) that are standing in your way when you
seek a relationship.

1. When I begin to reveal more about myself, I often
become afraid that the other person will reject me.
  Could be . . . *fear of intimacy*. When you become
interested in a person and find your feelings about that
person to be growing, the prospect of losing the relationship may become very threatening. Of course, one
way to protect yourself against loss is never to let
yourself get involved in the first place. While there is
never a guarantee that you will hold on to a cherished
relationship, neither will you ever have one if you don't
take the risk.

2. If things get too intimate and intense, I feel as
though I've lost control of the ability to direct my life.
  Could be . . . *fear of loss of control*. Like Eileen,
you may be concerned that if you really open up and
really get involved with someone—and really let that
person see who you are—then you will not be in control. But the suggestion is that not being in control
would be catastrophic. Mature love involves not losing
control of one's feelings or emotions, but choosing at

times to *relinquish* control while still standing on your own two feet.

3. I become too attached to the other person, and then begin to find the prospect of temporary or permanent separation too painful.

Could be . . . *clutchiness*. If you adopt the fear that you will lose the other person, you may get a little bit too clutchy, dependent, and possessive. This is an attitude you can change both by gaining greater confidence in the person or by reminding yourself that it will not be as catastrophic as you imagine if a separation does occur.

4. The degree to which I fall in love is something over which I have no control.

Could be . . . *love-proneness*. Someone who is love-prone *habitually* falls in love. If you are love-prone, you may believe that you have no control over your emotions in general and that you can catch love (at first sight) almost as if it were some kind of virus. Being love-prone can be a trap, and the way out of this trap is to learn that you have a choice as to whether you get involved emotionally or otherwise. Your heartfelt emotions are only *one* way in which you perceive, evaluate, and judge others. Your rational mind, of course, is different. See both points of view and then step back and decide what's best for you. You can choose to use your rational mind to *reduce* the intensity of your feelings if that's your choice.

5. When I really begin to adore someone, I panic and start having serious doubts about getting more deeply involved.

Could be . . . *love doubts*. First of all, remember that everyone probably has some doubts at one time or another. Make certain that you are not still mourning an old relationship or fearing that you will be scorned again in a manner that you once were. If you have unfinished business that existed before this relationship, it may come up again in the form of excessive doubts unless you take the responsibility to deal with that which is unresolved.

6. When someone is really very interested in me, I assume there must be something wrong with that person.

Could be . . . *low self-esteem.* You may be harboring the attitude that Groucho Marx summed up in the line "I'd never join a club that would have me as a member." If you believe that anyone who is interested in you must have gross defects and must be avoided, it is likely that you'll grow even more self-cynical. Ask yourself, "Am I good enough for the man or woman I want to meet?" If the answer is no, then the issue almost certainly is your self-esteem.

7. If I get into a relationship, I fear that I will lose my privacy or will have to give up parts of my single lifestyle that I enjoy.

Could be . . . *fear of loss of freedom.* The amount of freedom each person has within a relationship—and just what that freedom entitles a person to do—is something that is negotiable between the two people. In any relationship, it is important to know just what freedom *you're* willing to relinquish in order to make that relationship thrive.

8. If I show my commitment to the other person, the relationship is likely to take a turn for the worse.

Could be . . . *fear of commitment.* There is a possibility that a partner will turn out to be an entirely different person once you become more involved. On the other hand, you can take as much time as you need to explore the realities of the person to whom you are considering becoming committed. Most important, if you do make a mistake, it will be difficult, there will be many hassles, but it won't be the end of the world.

9. Everyone I get involved with seems to have something wrong with him (or her).

Could be . . . *perfectionism*. This can blunt your good sense when it comes to being realistic about the people you meet. Remember, relationships are made on earth, not in heaven. It is extremely unlikely that you'll find anyone who will fulfill *all* of your fantasies of what a soulmate should be. What you settle for is up to you, but the more stringent your requirements, the harder it will be to fill your order.

10. Whether or not I want to, I often suffer by comparing my current partner with one I had in a previous relationship.

Could be . . . *excessive partner comparison*. Comparing an eligible potential partner with a past partner can be a double-edged sword. Although some comparison is expected, if you previously have been rejected and are looking at your former partner through rose-colored glasses, your present partner is likely to come out looking quite unable to measure up. On the other hand, if you're looking at your former partner in a negative light, the present partner is likely to look unrealistically good by comparison.

11. I am afraid of someone finding out everything there is to know about me.

Could be . . . *fear of disclosure*. The assumption here is that you must disclose *everything* about yourself to your potential partner. That assumption may be based upon seeing your parents' relationship or from your own experience with previous relationships where you felt compelled to disclose a great deal about yourself. But you can use discretion and still be straightforward.

12. As soon as I get to know someone better, I start to lose interest in the relationship.

Could be . . . *in love with infatuation.* It may be that you are attracted to someone only until the relationship gets past the very first stages of initial attraction, infatuation, or lust. As soon as your curiosity is fulfilled, interest starts to wane. This is normal if it happens occasionally. But if it happens all the time, you may want to look at what it is that you fear about getting more deeply involved. Counseling or therapy could be helpful if you wish to break a recurring pattern of avoiding relationships.

13. I always act less interested than I actually am, so the other person cannot take advantage of me.

Could be . . . *game playing.* If you characteristically play the game of "hard to get"—by acting less interested than you actually are or by often acting standoffish toward the potential partners to the extent of pushing them away—you may be unwittingly expressing some feeling toward someone who hurt you in the past. Also, you may be convinced that playing "hard to get" keeps you more in control or makes you seem more attractive.

14. When a relationship turns sexual, I often wonder whether I'm being too aggressive—or not responsive enough.

Could be . . . *overplaying the importance of sex.* You may have convinced yourself that sex is all that's important. If so, you overplay the importance of initial sex in a relationship—and either disqualify someone who does not provide instant ecstasy, or who seems to want more of a sexual relationship than you do.

15. I'm afraid of my own ambivalence.

Could be . . . *fear of hurting your partner.* You may be very committed to the relationship that you have chosen psychologically—but at the same time you may fear that once you actually make the commitment that you both want, then you will be sorry and end up hurting the other person very deeply. This is a natural fear for practically everyone who has chosen to get into a new relationship. Don't panic! A very normal occurrence during courtship is to back off. Expect that your partner will do it as well. Think of it as a psychological dance that in most cases results in both of you testing the limits of the relationship.

16. I often seem to meet people who have *some* of the things I'm looking for in a partner—but not everything.

Could be . . . *creating the perfect (and artificial) partner.* If you imagine that there is a perfect person out there waiting for you, you may be putting together all the best characteristics of your previous partners to form an imaginary person whom you then seek out. It's unlikely that you will find one person who will fit *all* the specifications on your list.

17. I often get interested in a person who is involved in another relationship.

Could be . . . *"All-the-good-ones-are-taken" syndrome.* If you usually get involved with people who are married or are *un*available to you, it could be a sign that you consider availability a weakness.

18. Even when I have strong positive feelings about a

relationship at first, I eventually find myself saying or doing things specifically to test the other person.

Could be . . . *the vulnerability syndrome.* This may occur if you're the type of person who is capable of putting up a good, strong front when you meet someone, but as you begin to experience feelings, you become ultrasensitive. At this later stage you may be prone to constantly ask questions such as, "Do you really love me?" and to use practically any incident that comes up to test the relationship. At that point, you aren't coming across as the same person you were when your partner met you, and the relationship can become very strained.

Other Obstacles?

Apart from those obstacles with which you may have identified in the above Personal Profile, you could have another recognized emotional obstacle that isn't in any of these categories. If that is so, why not hold up the psychological mirror once again and try to identify the obstacle. Again, whether or not you seek ways to remove that obstacle is your choice—but, in any case, you have an advantage if you can see what it is.

Look at Relationships

What have you learned about your last relationship, or the one before that, from taking your Personal Profile? See if you can recognize some patterns of your own in that relationship that could have contributed to its demise.

While doing this, forget about how inappropriate the other person may have been. This learning exercise is for *your* benefit and yours alone. (I have rarely met a couple whose relationship ended merely because one of the partners was inappropriate or inept. Almost always, there was collaboration between the two.) Take a close look at your part in its ending. No one else has to know, but that truth could be crucial to your next relationship.

Talk to Some People

To complete this profile, I advise that you talk to some people who know you well. Ask for feedback. If you are still friends with someone you were in a relationship with, talk to that person. Ask for his or her perception of how you may have put barriers up. Don't do it in a threatening or confrontational way, but in a compassionate, gentle way that reinforces the other person's honesty.

We all have certain blind spots about ourselves. Characteristics that are glaring to other people may be things that we ourselves don't recognize.

Quite often people don't give us feedback because they believe it could hurt us, or they believe we don't want to hear it! Make yourself available for that feedback and you will prosper psychologically.

Note: if you are coming up with a blank when you try to think of someone you can turn to for feedback and frank discussion, you may wish to consider a professional counsellor or psychotherapist.

What If I Don't Want to Change?

You may be someone who is fond of saying to yourself, "I only want a partner who will accept me exactly the way I am." This is your right—but if this is what you believe, keep in mind that it is the other person's perfect right, as well, to pass you up.

Or perhaps you don't really want a relationship right

now; you're more interested in the chase—that great initial attraction—and you want the chase to continue. That is a choice—and if you have made it *your* choice, enjoy it until you become willing to put up with the lull and the little bit of boredom that comes after the chase. Almost always, long-term relationships do involve a period of lull and boredom. Though some can maintain the initial excitement while infatuation *turns* to love, I have *never* met anyone who was able to maintain the initial excitement indefinitely!

What Works for You?

Each of us has his or her own obstacles to overcome, but what about finding the other person? Where are—and who are—the potential partners that might be right for you if you are seeking a relationship? Do you have someone in mind, right now, who might be an *appropriate* partner for you?

Is there a possibility that there are many others you have not met who might turn out to be appropriate? And, if so, how can you go about finding them?

Or is it true, as some people claim, that all the good ones are taken?

Chapter 24

What Is an Inappropriate Partner?

Claire, a thirty-one-year-old administrative assistant, has been dating a married man. In many ways, she thinks that he is right for her and that the relationship feels very fulfilling. Warren is a successful and prominent investment banker who travels a great deal. Though he has been estranged from his wife for a number of years, he has kept the marriage together for the sake of his three children.

To Claire, Warren was living proof of the adage, "All the good ones are taken." When she first met him, she saw in him almost all the qualities that she appreciated in a man, and she has appreciated those qualities even more as their relationship has continued. Yet even though they are lovers, in most ways he is unavailable to her as long as he remains in his marriage. And at this point it does not seem likely that his status is going to change.

Right now, the relationship has many things that Claire feels she needs, and she is reluctant to move toward changing it or letting go. In his lovemaking

Warren is gentle, attentive, and intensely romantic. He sees her as frequently as his circumstances will allow, and he calls her often.

Warren has also been very supportive of Claire's goals. At the time they met, she was considering a career change. With his encouragement, she has started to take undergraduate courses in business management. She hopes to advance to a better position in her company.

Between work, study, and an active social life with her friends, Claire makes few demands on Warren's time. But whenever he is free, she seizes every available moment with him. Recently, she has begun to feel a need for a more committed relationship. But she has not discussed this need with him. There are no signs that he intends to divorce his wife and leave his family, and Claire does not want to jeopardize this passionate relationship that in many ways has made her very happy.

Claire knows that she has many relationship needs that Warren will be unable to fulfill. She is looking for commitment. She would eventually like to have children. She wants more companionship with her partner than Warren is able to provide. Yet she is too ambivalent to end the relationship—but not content the way it is.

Inappropriate Partners— Who Are They?

Practically every relationship will work at some level. A platonic friendship that is quite successful might become less so if the relationship turns sexual. An intimate sexual relationship might work as long as the partners are living separately—but dissolve unhappily if the partners try to move in together. Some relationships thrive as long as the two people see each other on an interim basis, but wane when one (or even both) of them mentions commitment.

Claire's relationship with Warren works as long as he is married *and* as long as she does not push him for a commitment. But who is to say what would happen if she made greater demands on him or if he did decide to seek a divorce and become more committed to Claire?

In love relationships, there is a natural tendency to want to elevate the relationship from occasional dates toward an exclusive dating relationship; then, perhaps, toward a relationship where you are together four, five, or six days a week. Finally, you may want to take the relationship to living together, then marriage, then having children.

But just because a relationship works at one level does not necessarily mean that it will work at another.

Though Claire found something in her relationship with Warren that was initially fulfilling, now she feels unsatisfied because the relationship cannot lead to a commitment. Like many people, Claire initially had emotional illusions about the person she loved.

Emotional Illusions

If you ever find yourself in relationships with people who are not appropriate for you, your problem could be one of *emotional illusions*.

For instance, you may see your relationship as being a very mature one when in fact it is characterized by a great deal of insecure and immature behavior. You might have the illusion of love, when what you actually are experiencing is infatuation. You could see a relationship moving toward commitment, when in fact it only works well as long as one or both partners remain distant, unresolved, or uncommitted.

Claire had an emotional illusion that being with Warren every day in a committed relationship would be as intense and special as it was to have an affair with him.

Partner Profile

When we begin to have illusions about a relationship, we may erroneously perceive an *inappropriate partner* as being an *appropriate partner*.

Who *is* an appropriate partner for you? How do you find out?

One way is to look at some of the dynamics of what is going on between you and someone you're currently involved with. Or ask yourself about a past relationship that did not work out for one reason or another.

The Partner Profile below includes fourteen first-person observations on relationships. In your notebook, make a list numbered 1 through 14. If the observation *does* describe your past or present relationship with someone, write YES alongside the number. If not, write NO.

An evaluation follows the Partner Profile.

PARTNER PROFILE

1. "Just when my partner and I seemed to be getting passionately involved, he/she suddenly pulled away. Now this person has become much less attentive and obviously wants to end the relationship."

    _____ YES, this describes my (past or present) relationship.

    _____ NO, this does not describe my relationship.

2. "I am seeing a person who has recently ended a marriage [or a long-term relationship]. This person wants to get very involved with me right away, even though that would mean turning a lot of my life upside down."

    ____ YES, this describes my (past or present) relationship.

    ____ NO, this does not describe my relationship.

3. "We began the relationship on a very mature, equal footing. But now it seems as if this person is only capable of thinking about his/her own needs."

    ____ YES, this describes my (past or present) relationship.

    ____ NO, this does not describe my relationship.

4. "Our relationship was fine until I began asking for a more committed involvement. Then he/she began to withdraw and act threatened."

    ____ YES, this describes my (past or present) relationship.

    ____ NO, this does not describe my relationship.

5. "I am involved with a person who is always very exciting to be with. This person enjoys fun, excitement, new challenges, a change of pace. But I'm beginning to think the relationship lacks stability."

    ____ YES, this describes my (past or present) relationship.

    ____ NO, this does not describe my relationship.

6. "I am having an intense, passionate relationship with someone who often seems like my perfect soul mate, but in reality our interests are so different that I wonder whether we really have anything in common."

    ____ YES, this describes my (past or present) relationship.

    ____ NO, this does not describe my relationship.

7. "I am involved with a married person. Even though my friends are warning me that 'it won't work out,' that relationship is fulfilling my needs."

    ____ YES, this describes my (past or present) relationship.

    ____ NO, this does not describe my relationship.

8. "I am seeing a person with whom I am very much in love. The person has not yet fallen in love with me, but I believe this will happen in time."

    ____ YES, this describes my (past or present) relationship.

    ____ NO, this does not describe my relationship.

9. "I am involved with a person who seems very nice, but he is very reluctant to talk about any past relationships. Also, he has a lot of free-floating anger that is extremely difficult to break through."

    ____ YES, this describes my (past or present) relationship.

    ____ NO, this does not describe my relationship.

10. "I keep meeting people who seem very interested in me as long as everything is going smoothly in the relationship. But as soon as I bring up an issue or concern, that person is likely to leave."

    _____ YES, this describes my (past or present) relationship.

    _____ NO, this does not describe my relationship.

11. "I am in a relationship with someone who I believe drinks too much. But when I have shown concern about it, that person either gets defensive or refuses to discuss it with me."

    _____ YES, this describes my (past or present) relationship.

    _____ NO, this does not describe my relationship.

12. "I have a good relationship with someone who is equally successful in his/her career. But whenever I mention a new achievement or accomplishment of my own, this person puts me down in some way."

    _____ YES, this describes my (past or present) relationship.

    _____ NO, this does not describe my relationship.

13. "I am very close to someone who seems to have different values in regard to family life."

    _____ YES, this describes my (past or present) relationship.

    _____ NO, this does not describe my relationship.

14. "I was in a relationship that was very intense and passionate for a while. Then, all of a sudden the other person seemed to lose interest."

_____ YES, this describes my (past or present) relationship.

_____ NO, this does not describe my relationship.

_____

EVALUATING YOUR PARTNER PROFILE

The dynamics in these relationships have been observed before in many cases—so you are not alone if you have been involved with a partner who seems or ultimately turns out to be inappropriate for you.

To gain some insight about the partner with whom you are involved—or have been involved with in the past—look below for the numbers that correspond to your YES responses.

1. Could be . . . *"conquer-and-control" syndrome.* These are people who may try to develop a relationship and stick around only until the other person is feeling passionately romantic. Although your partner may act as though he or she is equally vulnerable, your partner has real ambivalence about getting into romantic relationships. If it is a man, he may become sexually impotent. If it is a woman, she may simply flee the relationship.

2. Could be . . . *involvement with someone in a rebound relationship.* Rebound relationships rarely work in the long run because, often, the rebounder is trying to anesthetize his or her pain rather than acting on a genuine attraction and desire. Among the warning signs of a rebound relationship:

■ The person may expect you to let him or her move in right away, even though that could mean a major disruption of your own life.

■ The person always portrays his or her ex in negative terms, taking little or no responsibility for the failure of the previous relationship. This could indicate that your partner is either a chronic blamer (great reason to stay away, in itself), or is so entangled in the issues of the ended relationship that some anger from that relationship carries over when he or she is with you.

■ People who leave a relationship through no choice of their own may be too passive to take control of their own life. You might, therefore, become a crutch because such a person is afraid to go it alone.

■ Someone who is still longing for his or her ex is not ready to get involved with you in a serious way, regardless of what he or she may tell you.

3. Could be . . . *the illusion of maturity*. You may become highly attracted to someone you *perceive* as having a mature personality, and you see this individual as someone who can reciprocate. However, if the person is only capable of thinking about the fulfillment of his or her own needs, it is a sign that he/she does not have the maturity to sustain the relationship. There are many possible reasons for this. For example, it could be a fear of intimacy, a tendency to play games that will sabotage the relationship, or perhaps simple narcissism.

4. Could be . . . *fear of commitment*. A person who fears commitment cannot be pushed. The best way to deal with someone like this is to help your friend to fell *less* threatened—not more threatened or overwhelmed. If you back off a bit—that is, come on a bit less

strongly—then perhaps that person will come forward when he or she feels more comfortable.

5. Could be . . . *a problem with "balloons and strings."* In most relationships, balance is achieved because one person generally acts as the balloon and the other person as the string. The balloon is the person who is the dominant personality in the relationship—the one who most often makes things move. The string, on the other hand, is the one who brings stability to the relationship. A relationship with two balloons usually has no stabilizing force, and a relationship with two strings generally has little movement or excitement to it. In an ideal relationship, partners comfortably and automatically switch roles, depending on the particular aspect of the relationship and each partner's strengths and weaknesses.

6. Could be . . . *opposites attract.* Although opposites often do attract each other, the more you have in common with your new partner, the more chance the relationship has of sustaining itself beyond the infatuation phase. When you are first getting to know someone, it is a good idea to use creative ways to share interests or activities together and not rely on romance alone. A relationship may not get past that glorious burst of romantic passion unless you actually get to know your friend and still have positive feelings of liking that person.

7. Could be . . . *involvement with an unavailable person.* If you are one to whom freedom is the most important thing, and involvement with a married person does not seriously conflict with your own value system, then that arrangement may be right for you. If things are working well in the relationship, you may need to concede that it will work only as long as nothing changes—as long as your lover's spouse does

not begin to demand more time, or you do not decide that you are the odd one out and want more involvement. Frequently, if these changes do happen, the arrangement may come to an end—or may become a source of more pain than pleasure.

8. Could be . . . *a one-sided love affair.* One thing that is changing for the better is the acceptance of friendships between men and women in a platonic way. This could work fine unless one of you wants a more intense relationship with romance involved—in which case, it is likely to become an inappropriate relationship. Sometimes the result of this kind of involvement is a pseudosexual relationship where the person who would rather just be a friend allows the involvement to go beyond friendship and become sexual (in order to avoid rejection or to guard what is perceived as a valuable friendship). Unfortunately, it is improbable that the one who is less involved will change those feelings of friendship to feelings of romantic love. Also, it is extremely difficult to simply turn off inappropriate or unrequited feelings of love that you may have for the other person.

9. Could be . . . *a partner-hater.* A person who does not really like or respect his or her partner—which can happen for a variety of reasons—is quite often a person without a past, who is very reluctant to talk about other relationships in any meaningful way. That person may also have a generalized sense of anger that is very hard to get through. Unless the individual decides to change his pattern, it won't change. It is a mistake to think that *you* will change it.

10. Could be . . . *the replaceable-partner syndrome.* A person who sees having a partner as a *necessity* likes to have a partner always in place . . . until there are problems of any consequence in the rela-

tionship. Thus, as soon as an issue comes up, you are seen as someone who can be replaced easily by someone else. The relationship goes down with the first punch because this person is unwilling to work to resolve any issues. Many women have complained that, as a result of the "abundance of women" and "shortage of men," men are very likely to run away as soon as an issue comes up, rather than face it, because it's just as easy for them to find someone new as to deal with the issue.

11. Could be . . . *a substance abuser.* A substance abuser who denies having a drinking or drug problem—when you can observe that the use of the substance is obviously excessive or inappropriate—is someone who will turn out to be disappointing or downright heartbreaking in the end.

12. Could be . . . *a breeder of low self-esteem.* A partner who is happier when you feel inadequate than when you feel especially good about yourself, and one who devalues you when you achieve something, is usually someone who has low self-esteem. Particularly if you are an achiever or are ahead of your partner in your career, this insecure person may do everything possible to negate your success.

13. Could be . . . *classical incompatibility.* Values are deeply help beliefs about how life should be lived, and they usually don't change in a significant way. A person with entirely different values from yours with respect, say, to having children, is unlikely to change except as a result of a very gradual evolution, unless that person decides to make an intense effort to change.

14. Could be . . . *the "meteor syndrome."* This is the person who comes on strong, then fades away. The relationship goes up high and intense—and then, just

as quickly as it went up, it fizzles down. The partner in this kind of relationship is constantly seeking new high levels of excitement and will soon move on to another person.

Choosing Partners

If you are concerned that a number of relationships have not worked for you in the past because your partners were inappropriate in similar ways, you might compare your Personal Profile (Chapter 23, page 165) with the Partner Profile above. There are elements in your own emotional obstacle course that mean you are more attracted to one kind of partner than another. If that partner shares the level of involvement that you want, then in all probability, this an appropriate partner for you. But if the relationship is not working for you—or if you want a deeper level of commitment—you may want to consider ways of changing the patterns that could be leading you to inappropriate partners.

A perfectly good person (for someone else) can be totally inappropriate for you in a relationship. The two of you may look good on paper, and you may have a lot in common, but you still have no chemistry in common. Remember, *there is no way to induce desire if it is not there*. On the other hand, the lack of desire on either side does not mean that one or the other of you is to blame.

Pushing Toward Commitment

Pushing toward commitment can sometimes have the paradoxical effect of hurting some relationships that work at one level but not the next. I have seen very good friendships come apart because one of those involved tried to elevate the relationship to involvement on a more intimate level.

Just because you are good friends does not mean that you will be great lovers.

Just because you are good lovers does not mean that you should become *steady* lovers.

Of course, sometimes, escalating the relationship *does* work. So if you think it can, sure—give it a try—take the risk.

But if you find that your relationship has become too involved, or is not working at a more intense level, you might consider *downgrading* it. I have known many ex-husbands and ex-wives who simply could not get along well as spouses, but found that they became *very* good friends after separation or divorce.

The Hold-out Option

There are many singles who choose to exercise the *hold-out option*. If you are comfortable living alone, you may choose singlehood. You have the benefit of being able to wait and see—enjoying warm, supportive friendships and nonromantic relationships on many different levels—without putting your energy into the search for a more intimate relationship or long-term commitment.

You may decide that the hold-out option is the right choice for you at this point in your life and that it is a lot less painful than a relationship that involves stifling compromise.

Chapter 25

Is Anything Stopping You?

Making the effort to meet people means taking risks, and it could also mean getting rejected. Fear of rejection is common, but that fear gets expressed in different ways, depending on the individual. Often, fear of rejection is expressed as shyness. But fear of rejection can also be acted out in the form of overconfidence—coming on so strong that the other person is almost blown away.

When you take a risk with someone, you are actually putting yourself in a no-lose situation. When you approach someone new, only two things can happen: you might meet someone new, or you might be rejected. Either way, you're a winner. If the person responds to your interest, then you've improved your odds in the numbers game. And if that person is *not* interested, what is the *worst* thing that can happen to you? What if you are rejected by somebody you have never met or by someone who has not yet had the chance to become important to you? Is it really that big a deal? Every time you get rejected, you are proving that rejection is something you can stand. So is it worth putting your social life on hold just to avoid that eventuality?

Emotional Fire Drill

One way to overcome the fear of rejection is to *play out an emotional fire drill,* imagining the worst thing that could happen to you. For example, let's say there's somebody to whom you are very attracted, and this person turns out to reject you. At the most extreme, that person might turn around and walk away—or say something like "I'm really not interested in talking to you."

But let's take a much more likely scenario—a polite but firm rejection. Can you handle that? See if you can *practice feeling that rejection* and then *think through what alternatives you have.*

The *emotional fire drill* scenario might go like this:

YOU: "Would you like to have lunch tomorrow."

THE OTHER PERSON: "I'm sorry, I can't. I have a meeting at noon."

YOU: "How about sometime next week?"

THE OTHER PERSON: "Next week is very busy for me. We have sales conference coming up, and I have to get ready."

Now what do you do? Some alternatives . . .

YOU MIGHT REPLY: "That sounds like a nice break. Where are they holding it this year?" (Never mind pushing lunch right now. Get to know the person better, and if the chemistry seems to improve, you might try to set a date later.)

OR YOU MIGHT REPLY: "Well, I hope we can get together. Here's my card. If you'd like to, give me a call when your sales conference is over." (Very direct, but you put the ball in the other court.)

OR YOU MIGHT REPLY: "Let me call in a couple of weeks when your schedule is clear." (Still pushing for the lunch date. Shows determination, but are you pushing too hard?)

Whichever reply you choose, there is one basic rule of thumb. Put yourself in the other person's place. Then consider which reply would seem appropriate to *you* in that person's place.

Now, look back on this emotional fire drill. What really happened? You took a risk—asking the other person to lunch—and you got an evasive reply that you may or may not take as a rejection.

Was it really so bad? Were you that hurt by the other person's reply? Even if you never get together, have you truly lost something of value?

There could be a host of reasons why this individual was not receptive to you. An involvement with someone else? Specific tastes that are not compatible with yours? Perhaps you tapped into his or her own anxiety or shyness; in fact, right after rejecting you, this person might have wondered why he or she couldn't be positively receptive to you. And, yes, it's possible that you are not what that person considers someone to spend time with, or maybe the other person found you downright unattractive.

Give yourself a positive message: "Just because this individual did not respond to me as I wanted, it does not mean there is something wrong with me." Once you've been able to bring yourself out of a negative state of mind in rehearsal, you'll find that it can be done when the real thing occurs as well.

Imagine *you will find a way to get yourself through the crisis*. Then, believe me, when it really happens you will probably be able to recover quickly from the negative effects of rejection.

It is the fear of being unable to cope with the situation that makes that phantom fear of rejection so real. With a little practice you can toughen yourself up to rejection and start looking at it as a mere hassle rather than a horror.

In fact, one of my favorite homework assignments is to have people go out and actually *get* rejected two times in one week, just to make them less sensitive to rejection. I tell them that in this homework assignment, successes don't count. Ironically, it almost always takes a lot of successful interaction to get the two rejections. With a little bit of practice, you'll never fear that rejection again.

Other Roadblocks

Fear of rejection is not the only thing that prevents one person from meeting another. There are other roadblocks that might be preventing you from taking the first step:

PHONY PHOBIA

Some people fear that they will be phony unless they are *totally* honest about themselves. So rather than encounter someone to whom they'd feel obliged to tell all, they avoid meeting in the first place.

Derek avoided what he called "the party scene" for that reason:

> I can't pretend I'm someone with a lot of money and class. I work hard, I do okay, but I'm not the

kind of guy who's going to sweep a woman off her feet, because I don't know how to do that. Why should I pretend? If I try to act like a phony, some woman is just going to get the idea that the phony guy is the real me.

Rather than take the risk of hiding anything, Derek began to avoid social situations altogether. In group counseling, however, he practiced some role-playing that gradually convinced him it could be fun to try different approaches to people. The responses of other people in the group helped to remind him that people in social situations usually did not take these encounters as seriously as he was taking them. Once he felt he had some choices about how he came across to people, he actually began to enjoy mingling.

Laura, another member of the group, realized she had a slightly different kind of phony phobia. Soon after meeting someone new, she found herself telling that person more than she really wanted to, and ended up abasing herself before the person really got to know her very well.

Like Derek, Laura was actually afraid to hide anything. She thought that to tell anything but the whole truth was to be phony—and to be phony was to be a horrible person. So in trying to be the "real Laura," she ended up actually describing her worst characteristics or putting herself down.

My experience is that if you show all your warts too early in the game, you can turn off a very worthwhile person. So what is the answer?

At first, give at the very least a picture of yourself that errs in a positive direction if it errs at all. My experience is that people who insist on revealing too much too soon—in the name of being "real" or "unphony"—are people who are most likely afraid to get involved at all. They in reality secretly sabotage themselves by doing whatever they can to turn the other person off.

CONVERSATION ANXIETY

This is often caused by the fear of seeming foolish or awkward and of being rejected. The key here is to take the pressure off yourself by getting the other person to talk. Almost always, you can keep the conversation going by asking open-ended questions that encourage the other person to talk. Questions beginning with "How . . .?" "Why . . .?" or "What do you think . . .?" *open up* the conversation. "How did you find an apartment?" "What did you do in Jamaica?" "What do you think will happen in the Middle East?"

SCREENING

Sometimes, when first meeting a person of the opposite sex, you may expect some signal that he or she is right for you or almost instantly attracted to you. What do you do if the signals aren't there?

When I asked this question on the air, a caller named Marjorie offered what I thought were some excellent suggestions for listeners:

> It took me a while to realize why I was always meeting the wrong kind of men. The type of guy I like is basically pretty quiet and considerate—I don't mean boring, but just kind of low-key. But that's always the hardest kind of guy to get to know, because he might not say much or show much the first time you meet him. So if I were looking for instant electricity, I would end up with Flashy Dan—you know, the smooth guy at the bar who always has a great line and after about ten minutes tells you how wonderful you are.

Then I realized I would have to have some patience if I were going to meet the kind of man I wanted to meet. Now, if I meet someone nice, I don't screen him out just because he's quiet or serious at first. And I don't assume that he's *not* interested in me just because it may take him a while to warm up.

Someone who is shy or reticent needs encouragement. With someone like that, you need to look for the subject that will strike a spark. That's not always easy. It takes some looking. But no one can resist a compliment. I try to find out—from someone else, if necessary—what that person has done. Then I lead with a comment or compliment about whatever it is that interests him: "I understand you restore antique furniture. I admire that. When someone puts a lot of care into restoration, it really shows."

If I want a date with that person when I get to know him better, I might have to take the initiative. Shy people think, "If I ask her, she'll say 'No.'" I'll try to connect with something we've been talking about. "You mentioned the antique auction. I'd like to go and bid—but I wouldn't know what's valuable. If I meet you there, maybe you can guide me."

Marjorie has said it all. It appeared she had expanded her tolerance level to meet some of the "diamonds in the rough" that a person is likely to find in almost any social situation. As she observed, shy people often get a lot better the more you get to know them—but it can take a while!

CONCERN WITH WHAT YOUR FRIENDS THINK

Doreen is a single woman who socializes a great deal and always seems to meet and make friends easily. I asked her what she considered the key to her success. "The silliest thing in the world," she replied. "I have no fear of public opinion. There's no one I'm trying to impress with myself. I don't go out with guys because I have to show my girl friend that I have this kind of guy or that kind of guy. I don't really give a damn. I'm there to please myself at all times. And I don't care what my friends think of my choices. If they don't like the guys I'm with, what kind of friends are they, anyway?"

If you have been allowing your friends' opinions to stand in the way of meeting people, you might reconsider. It's who *you* want to be with that really matters.

The Singles Scene

For some people, that very expression—"the singles scene"—conjures up a questionable environment specifically designed for the frantic pursuit of partners. For others, the scene is whatever they want to make of it. If the singles scene, for you, means meeting other people with whom you might become involved, it might encompass everything from your grandmother's kitchen to a punk-rock club downtown.

To get a sampling of ways you might meet the person you want to meet, consider the following:

Personal introduction. Most feel that this is by far the best way to meet people—but not always available because it assumes that your friends and family know other people whom you'd like to meet. If you've been single for a while, you may have to remind them that you're looking. And describe the kind of person you're looking for. Often, our friends—and especially our relatives—may think a certain kind of individual is perfect for us, when that type is exactly wrong. But they'll never know what you *do* want unless you tell them!

A no-lose situation. By a no-lose situation, I mean that by going places where you can do the things you enjoy, you will have a good time whether you meet someone or not. Maybe you would enjoy playing tennis or racquetball, joining book discussion groups, or singing in a Gilbert and Sullivan opera. If an activity like this is something you would enjoy *whether or not you are looking for a relationship,* then you're on the right track to a no-lose situation. There's an added benefit here, too: when you are doing what you enjoy, you look and feel your best.

Personal ads. If you have not already done so, you might look at the sample personal ad in Part Four, page 213 and then, as an experiment, try writing one of your own. Once you have it down on paper, take a look at it. Is this you? Does this sound like someone you would like to meet if it were written by your counterpart of the opposite sex?

As a next step, you might want to try the experiment of placing your personal ad in a reputable magazine where you may have seen personals that caught *your* interest. A steadily growing number of people have been successful in meeting partners through the personals. And you might be surprised at the quality of the responses. All those responses go to a box number, so you never have to answer them if you don't want to. At the very worst, you will spend a few dollars and not necessarily meet anyone worthwhile. At best, you might be successful in meeting someone this way—as many other people have been!

Networking. Networking for a relationship is a lot like networking for a new job. This can be done in several ways:

- Associating with business groups and professional activities
- Joining a singles network in your area
- Joining a group that works on community or social causes, bringing together people with a variety of expertise

Of course, you also have your own network consisting of friends' friends, and their friends. Let your circle expand from what may be a small nucleus to a much larger number of people. Networking is simply allowing the ripple effect to take place.

Dating services. While all dating services will claim that they have extensive lists of people who want to meet you, you have to pay your fee to find out. The best procedure is to use a dating service that has been recommended *by someone you know or trust who has successfully met someone else through the service.* If you walk in cold, you have no way of knowing how many clients subscribe to that service, which ones are legitimate, and which are rip-offs.

Clubs. Select those that accommodate your interests. There are clubs for cycling, scuba diving, tennis, bowling, hang gliding, Ping-Pong, squash, soccer, racquetball, chess, checkers, and backgammon. *Any* special interest—any *slight* special interest—makes you eligible for a club. There are clubs for book lovers, music lovers, art lovers, cardplayers, vegetarians, and crossword-puzzle lovers. Other clubs to consider: ethnic, religious, professional, political; clubs for the disabled and handicapped; clubs for people over sixty-five or under twenty-five; clubs for drivers (one in Chicago is called "Street-Hearts"); clubs for special causes (save trees, clean the air, plant gardens); clubs for tall people, short people, overachievers, and geniuses.

Sporting events. If it's men you want to meet, a good place to go may be male-oriented sporting events—baseball games, football games, skeet shooting, fly-fishing, karate competitions.

Classes. Adult learning centers are springing up all around the country; numerous high schools sponsor adult educational programs; organizations promoting music, drama, and the arts sponsor all kinds of classes, lectures, and tours; museums have classes; and YMCAs, YMHAs, and YWCAs have numerous courses. The class you are likely to choose will probably depend on your personal tastes (for a no-lose situation, as described above), but if you are a man, you probably cannot do better than to sign up for a cooking class; and no woman who is interested should hesitate to take car repair or cabinetry.

Co-ed health clubs. If singles bars were the place to meet people in the late sixties and the seventies, health clubs have all but replaced them. There are an estimated four thousand commercial racquet and fitness clubs around the country. According to one survey, 77 percent of the members in these clubs are single adults.

Again, a no-lose situation. You will certainly get the health benefits whether you meet someone or not.

Singles bars. Yes, singles bars. Many happy relationships and marriages grew out of first meetings in singles bars—and, naturally, those people recommend them highly. Others, who have met with steady disappointment or frustration, would recommend otherwise.

But there are some people who really enjoy going to a singles bar whether they meet someone or not, because they may go with their own group of friends and just have a good time.

Several observations apply, however. The population in a singles bar usually includes not just singles but also a number of married people. Since the people in the bar are not brought together by any common interest, keep in mind that you may be putting yourself among those with whom you have very little in common.

The other observation about singles bars, as we all know, is that people often put on what they think will be a marketable personality, rather than act as they do normally. You may have had a long conversation at a singles bar with a seemingly interesting partner who turns out to be quite a different person in another context—or when sober.

If you enjoy going somewhere for a drink, but singles bars tend to intimidate you, why not try a friendlier, more informal atmosphere—maybe the type of place that people frequent after work, or perhaps a private club. You may find a big difference.

Vacation and travel. Your vacation is a wonderful time to meet other singles, share activities you enjoy, and explore new horizons. Some of the possibilities to consider:

■ Tours and cruises. If you're going with a tour group, choose one that is specially designed for those who are single and are traveling alone. The majority of tour and cruise packages are priced for double occupancy, and the single traveler may have to pay a single supplement fee that is 50 to 75 percent higher than the per-person rate for people traveling as couples. But there are special tours for singles that give you a break on the price, and some can match you up with a companion who will share accommodations for the trip. Usually, you fill out a questionnaire about yourself and the travel companion you're looking for. Profiles are published in a newsletter. Many clubs advise that you take a short weekend trip with your prospective partner before you commit to sharing accommodations on a tour.

Some cruise lines offer roommate-sharing plans. (There may be a small surcharge for two singles in a double cabin.) A few cruise lines are designing single cabins for as many as 10 percent of their passengers, with no surcharge for those traveling alone.

■ Vacation clubs. There are many for singles, and some are better than others. Try to get a recommendation from someone whose judgment you trust.

■ A vacation house. Is there a house within driving distance that you can share as a weekend retreat? This is a terrific way to meet members of the opposite sex in a relaxed setting. If you are sharing the rental with others, try to meet some of their friends—these are the people *they* are likely to invite to the house.

■ World adventure and travel. Travel agencies are inundated with brochures for travel vacations of all kinds. Other good sources of information are magazines like *Smithsonian, Tours & Resorts, Travel and Leisure,* and *Natural History,* which frequently list organizations that run adventure and travel expeditions. Numerous adventure tours give you the opportunity to meet men and women who have a similar zest for adventure.

■ History, culture, and education. Many educational tours and vacations give you the opportunity to immerse yourself in a bygone civilization, learn a new subject, or improve your language skills. There are archaeology digs in the continental United States, as well as Mexico, Peru, Italy, Judaea, Greece, Crete, and many other locations. Universities sponsor short-term courses in various subjects: you can study English language and history at Oxford, pursue Celtic studies in Ireland and Scotland, brush up on French at the Sorbonne, or study the Renaissance in Florence. Many tours focus on cultural activities, such as theater, music, or opera. You will be with a group of people who share your interests and enthusiasms.

■ Outdoor sports and recreation. Numerous clubs, camps, and resorts cater to sports enthusiasts. Ask friends for recommendations, or write to resorts that are listed in a sports-related publication (*Golf Digest, Sail, Tennis World*, etc.). Some sports camps are specifically for singles.

Advice for Vacationing Singles

Philadelphia travel consultant Kiki Olson, who often travels solo, suggests that it's better to travel alone if you want to meet someone new, rather than take your best friend along. According to Kiki:

Traveling with your best friend often doesn't work. You have a tendency to be joined at the hip. You don't go out and push yourself into meeting other people. If you're traveling with a friend, you not only have to meet someone *you* like, but someone who matches up to your friend's expectations. And if your friend hasn't met someone and you have—what are you going to do?

My rule of thumb is, if you haven't been able to meet anyone in your home town while you were going to things with this person, the odds are you're not going to meet anyone on a *trip* when you're with that same person.

Kiki advises that the most important thing is that you do something you're interested in. "Whether it's scuba diving, archaeology, jazz, classical music, or horseback riding, go where you're comfortable, where you're interested in something, where you can speak intelligently about it, and where other people are interested in the same thing. You'll just meet more people that way."

Above all, she believes it's important to go with the right attitude if you want to meet someone. "Don't go with expectations," she says. "See it as a learning experience, and meet everyone you can. You may not meet the love of your life, but you can meet a lot of people. Consider it an adventure."

Positives Attract

Wherever you meet someone, *how*ever you meet someone, you will generally move more easily toward a relationship if you are meeting that person for positive rather than negative reasons. What are the positives? They could be . . .

- The desire to share your life with another person
- A desire for sensual or sexual pleasure
- Enjoyment of the presence of someone in whose company you have an unmistakable sense of well-being
- Enjoyment of the feelings that come from giving to another person when you are in a relationship

Positive reasons are characterized by *desire,* not fear or need.

Negative reasons, on the other hand, may be:

- The relief of loneliness

- The need to lessen feelings of low self-esteem that you may have about yourself for not being in a relationship
- The need to establish financial security
- The belief that those who are part of a couple are more valued than those who are not
- The need to get even by making your former partner jealous of your new one
- In order to get out of or over your last relationship

A relationship based on fear or need may fulfill *some* of your unmet desires, but too often it will only mask your pain temporarily. Conversely, if you want to meet someone in order to share yourself with that person, and vice versa—a *positive* desire—you are much more likely to find a solid, long-term relationship.

Relationships are likely to come more easily if you have the attitude that you are not in dire *need* of the person you are meeting, but that you would *like* to meet that person in order to enhance both of your lives.

Part Four

Getting Involved and Nurturing a Relationship

Chapter 26

If Your Goal Is Involvement

This chapter is designed for those of you who have chosen to seek involvement in a relationship. It can be referred to at any time—so that if you decide to leave the singles scene, you will have a place to begin. It's best to look upon the task of involvement as pragmatically as possible—beginning with the *most* pragmatic aspect of all, the numbers game.

The Numbers Game

Recognizing and meeting an appropriate person with whom to become involved is, like it or not, a numbers game. The more you take this task into your own hands, the more necessary it is to think in terms of meeting a *lot* of people.

One error that many people make in searching for an appropriate partner is in trying to make *whomever* you happen to meet into "the one." It would be very unusual indeed to find an appropriate partner at the first shot. So the more effort you put into meeting different people and exploring the potential for relationships with them, the better your chances of finding the one who will fill as many of your needs as possible. (And remember, although a relationship is only as good as the needs it fulfills, just about no relationship will fulfill all of your needs!)

If you refuse to take affirmative action in meeting a lot of people—and, instead, put it in the hands of fate and wait to be discovered—your mathematical chances of finding people with whom you can become involved obviously diminish. Many people say, "I finally met someone when I stopped looking."

I am not going to argue in favor of either position for you. I can only tell you from my own experience that I am an impatient person—and when there is something I want, I feel much better when I'm doing whatever I can do to improve my chances of getting it.

By taking the matter into your own hands, I believe you improve your chances. But the approach you use must be one of your own choosing or, ultimately, it probably will not work for you.

What Are My Chances?

What if you agree with people who say that it's fruitless even to try?

Perhaps you have heard recently that there are far more available single women than men. Many surveys have shown that, from a statistical point of view, this is true. The population as a whole has more women than men, and since men usually are more comfortable involving themselves with younger women than are women with younger men, time is not on the side of women. Also, men are (again, statistically) more apt to involve themselves with more than one person at a time than are women. Thus, several studies tend to support the view that the numbers game favors men. As one female caller on my program said: "How can I feel optimistic about meeting someone I want to marry? In just about every age group, single women outnumber single men, so men have a significant advantage. I may *want* to get married, but what can I do about the statistics? The probabilities are against me."

The reality is that there are several important factors—unacknowledged by the statisticians—that make the *usefulness* of the statistics somewhat questionable:

1. More women than ever before are staying single by *choice*. So if you are among those *wanting* to get married, your chances are improved considerably. So just wanting to get married could increase your chances many times—on just that *one* factor alone.

2. Your attitude affects your chances! To take the most extreme example—suppose you have decided that you're not looking for a spouse. That attitude alone reduces your chances of finding a spouse.

Or let's suppose that you are looking for a spouse with a very unusual combination of traits—for example, a very artistic person who is also financially secure. If that's the only kind of person you would consider a desirable partner, your chances of marrying might be closer to 1 to 2 percent.

On the other hand, if you are actively looking for a spouse, if you are willing to be somewhat flexible about your expectations and to work on obstacles that stand in your way, your chances could be closer to 99 or 100 percent.

Attitude can make a tremendous difference. So if the numbers in a statistical study sound pessimistic, remember that *they don't predict anything at all*. If you are using any kind of statistical study to make a negative prediction for yourself, then you run the risk of making it a self-fulfilling prophecy.

3. Trends can start tomorrow that might not be measurable for several years. For example, although divorced men now tend to have second marriages with women who are much younger, trends may soon change so that they start marrying successful never-married women who are older. Statistics of social change have always suffered from the dilemma that by the time a study is published, the trend is changed.

It can be unwise to allow statistics to dictate your personal behavior. Instead of saying, "I have not yet found the person whom I desire, but I will keep trying," someone who goes only by the statistics may say, "I have not yet found the person I desire because he/she does not exist, and I can prove it by the numbers!" If you adopt the attitude that it's hopeless (as opposed to difficult), you may stop trying and resolve that you will accept defeat, regardless of how important an area of your life this is.

Even in the upper age groups, where single women outnumber single men by as much as ten to one, it is largely your own decision as to whether you will give up trying out of a belief that it is fruitless—or stay in the race and be one of those who does find a relationship. The statistics present the likelihood of a greater challenge, but they do not provide an excuse to give up. Ironically, I have talked to many people who managed to find the very relationship they wanted *before* hearing it was an "impossibility."

Who Am I Looking For?

In the Attitude Inventories in Part Three, you had the opportunity to evaluate some of your own preferences in the matters of *Living Alone/Seeking a Relationship* (page 150) and *Personal Criteria: Whom Would You Consider as a Potential Partner?* (page 153). If you completed the inventories, I suggest you refer back to them now. Since these inventories reflect *your* personal preferences, reviewing them may serve as a reminder of why you are seeking a relationship at this time, of the criteria that you have chosen to use in considering a potential mate, and of the ways you might choose or not choose to look for potential partners.

If you have not already completed the inventories, turn to them now, before reading ahead in this chapter. Having a clearer view of your own preferences can be helpful in seeing the choices that are available to you if you are seeking a relationship. It can help you determine for yourself *why* you are seeking another person, *whom* you are looking for, and *where* you might go to find that person.

Just to give yourself a small exercise in self-assessment—what if you wanted to write a personal ad, based upon how you see yourself and what you want? Could you do it? And if so, how would it read?

Writing a Personal Ad for Practice

Man (38) seeks female companion (30–40) to share comfortable lifestyle. 5'8", excellent shape (I was All-College tennis champ), I have my own management consulting firm and have been in business for myself for three years. Compulsive worker but rarely travel and my Saturday nights are yours. I like the Grateful Dead, hate opera, wish the Beatles were still around. If you are an attractive professional woman who would rather eat take-out than be tied to the kitchen, you could be the one. Smokers need not apply.

It's amazing how much you can tell about a person from a single paragraph. Reading this typical personal ad—and reading between the lines—you can probably get a fairly good idea of this person's lifestyle, his tastes, his attitude toward women, his physique, his income, and his personal priorities. It's quite possible for a reader to get some idea about her compatibility with this person, even without meeting him.

If you have never written a personal ad, I recommend that you try it, not necessarily because you will ever choose to place this ad, but just for practice. Suppose, in ten lines or less, you have to give a thumbnail description of yourself—your most attractive characteristics, your likes and dislikes, your lifestyle, your tastes in members of the opposite sex, and any qualifications for a potential partner. Could you do it?

Let's look again at this personal and see what it tells us in very few words:

". . . seeks female companion . . ." Not every man would say "companion." He could have said, "seeks raven-haired beauty" or "seeks sensuous female." If he had, wouldn't you have a different impression of the man?

". . . comfortable lifestyle . . ." Not "fantastic" or "stimulating." There's nothing here to indicate that he's incredibly rich, but on the other hand, the word "comfortable" really does tell you something about the way he lives.

". . . compulsive worker . . ." Depending on the kind of mate you're seeking—and the kind of life *you* lead—this could be an asset or a drawback. By *telling* you he's a compulsive worker, you know his work is important to him, and he's not going to give it up. Also, chances are he'll give you the same freedom to pursue your line of work.

". . . I like the Grateful Dead, hate opera . . ." If you want to think about living with this person, you can literally hear the background music. Is it music that *you* would enjoy? Often, it's the small preferences that give you large clues to a person's character. Would you *share* those preferences?

". . . attractive professional woman . . ." You can see the image he has in his mind. Is this your image of yourself? Or would you have to remold yourself to fit the person that this man is looking for?

How to Meet People

The choice is now up to you. You can take a wait-and-see approach and hope that "the right person" comes along—or you can *actively* seek out your next relationship.

Waiting for lightning to strike is what I sometimes call the "Schwab's Drugstore" approach. Schwab's Drugstore is the Hollywood landmark where Lana Turner was discovered. She was sitting at the now-extinct counter, sipping a soda, when a producer came up to her and said, "You're exactly what we're looking for?" That day, a star was born!

At the other extreme is the Active Search approach. The idea of this is to increase your chances in a number of different ways:

1. *Set a goal of meeting a hundred people.* This is playing the numbers game. The more people you meet, the more you increase your chances of meeting someone who might be appropriate for you.

Kevin is a young draftsman in a small architectural firm. He literally works in the basement of the company, and he might go through a whole day without seeing anyone other than the secretary and one or two of the architects. He is not a naturally outgoing person anyway, so it seems to him that meeting people is becoming more difficult rather than less so. Yet he is ready to find a wife and have children. How can he break the pattern that is keeping him essentially isolated from potential partners?

At first Kevin thought I was kidding when I suggested that he actually meet a hundred women. But after we talked about how it was done, it didn't seem so unrealistic. I told Kevin to bring me a list of twenty-five places to go or things to do where there would be even the remotest chance of meeting a woman. If he went two places every week, and met one woman in each place, by the end of the year he would have met a hundred!

Once Kevin had the assignment, he began to think creatively about things he could do, places he could go, and ways he could meet people. Among some of the things he did during the year:

■ Talking with an architect in the firm, he found out about the annual Beaux-Arts Ball. He had been curious about the event—a full-regalia costume ball on Halloween night—but he'd never gone. The architect got Kevin an invitation and also mentioned the name of a designer in the firm who was interested in going. Kevin invited her. During their spare time at the office, they sketched and planned their costumes. Their costumes were a hit, and Kevin met about a dozen people in one night.

■ He called a cousin who lived in town, worked at an employment agency, and rented a summer house at the shore. Kevin told her he was trying to meet people. She invited him to the shore for the weekend, where he met a houseful of guests. She also got him an invitation to her neighbor's party. Between the two events, Kevin got to know five or six people fairly well.

■ From a listing in the back of a city magazine, he found out about a singles network for young professionals, and joined. The network sent out a monthly newsletter listing lectures, seminars, discussion groups, day hikes, and similar activities. Kevin made it his goal to attend at least one activity each week.

■ He joined the skiing club, which sponsored about a dozen trips during the season. During the winter, Kevin got to meet twenty single women on the various ski trips.

Kevin met Amy very briefly at the Beaux-Arts Ball, but he remembered her—and she remembered him—when they met again, about four months later, at one of the day-walks sponsored by the professional-singles network. They began dating steadily, and within a year they were engaged.

Although she was among the first people Kevin met when he started his assignment, she was also about the ninety-ninth—and it was only when he saw her again that they started going out. Kevin told me he was shy with people at parties—there were certain barriers he had trouble breaking through. But he didn't give up! Though it was tough going at first, by sticking to the plan, he achieved his goal!

He also got a side benefit from what started out as a kind of exercise for him: he got better at mingling with people in general and making friendships.

2. *Consider your criteria.* In the Attitude Inventory, you evaluated certain criteria that you applied to yourself and to potential partners. Can some of these criteria change? To the extent that you have a large number of specific criteria that other people must fulfill, you are limiting your field of choice. So if you can make some of those criteria optional without compromising your own standards, you could increase your range of choices.

One evening when we were discussing this topic on my radio program, a caller named Ava said she had always dated men who were taller than she was. She said this "policy" really began during high school years, because she had always felt embarrassed and conspicuous when she towered over the boys she dated. Later on, she simply assumed that most men were intimidated being with women who were taller than they were.

If she had stuck to that policy, she added, she would never have met the man with whom she was now having a very happy relationship. She said she had met him through his personal ad (which neglected to mention his height). She was shocked when someone four inches shorter showed up for their first meeting. But they had a wonderful evening, and their involvement grew from there.

Ava said she probably would not have even considered him an eligible candidate if she had seen him before she dated him. She said it was likely she would have written him off right away—just because he was too short!

Despite the fact that many of *your* criteria for appropriate partners may be more serious than this, it might be interesting to review the Attitude Inventory II (page 153), where you listed your criteria. Ask yourself which items are negotiable. Again, the purpose of this exercise is not to compromise what is important to you, but to see where you might broaden your range of choices by identifying areas of greater flexibility.

3. *What will you do to meet someone?* In Chapter 25, you had the opportunity to consider a range of choices regarding ways of meeting people—choices ranging from singles bars to a blind date arranged by relatives (page 198 forward). One way to increase the number of people you meet is by increasing the number of *ways* in which you could meet them.

One night, on a call-in program, I asked people who felt they were in happy relationships to call in and tell me where they had first met their partners. Their responses gave listeners an idea of the wide range of options that are available:

"I always thought singles bars were meat racks," said one caller. "I still don't believe I met the guy I married in one of those places. But I got into a group of women who were going there about once a week—and one night when I was there with my friends, he was there, too, and we started talking."

"I thought bird-watchers were all graying grandmothers," said a male caller. "But someone told me there were a lot of young women who were bird-watchers. I figured, Why not? There must be worse things than watching the sun rise with a bunch of young ladies looking for yellow warblers. As it turned out, that's how Cindy and I met."

"I got so sick of my mother saying I should meet this woman that I finally said, 'Okay, Mom, introduce us,'" another man said. "I was prepared for the worst. You know mothers. But it was a great choice: I liked the woman right away. If someone said to me, 'Don't listen to your relatives,' I'd have to say, 'Well, maybe that's true *most* of the time. But in this case . . .'"

And a woman: "I like tennis, but I never used to watch matches. I thought it would be boring. But I'd told myself I was going to meet some new men, and this was one way. So I went. It wasn't boring, so I went again. I think it was a break in the third match when I met Tom . . ."

A woman: "I was cross-country skiing. I was going downhill, he was coming up and was blocking the trail, so I had to stop. We started talking . . ."

A man: "Men aren't supposed to take cooking classes. But I took a cooking class. I had to cook for myself anyway, so I figured I might as well learn how with a lot of eligible women around me. Susan and I had to chop the vegetables together. That's how . . ."

A woman: "It was an all-male softball team. But I told them I could play first base . . ."

A woman: "My personals ad just said I liked ballroom dancing and wanted a partner . . ."

A man: "Oxford University runs this stuffy summer program called Introduction to the Classics. I've always liked the idea of Oxford, and I had two weeks off, so . . ."

The calls didn't stop coming for a full hour—and I don't think there were two callers who described meeting their partners in the same way. If there were themes to that show, they could be summed up in the words "risk," "luck," and "ingenuity."

4. *And if you're into efficiency* . . . Not long ago, a female executive in Washington, D.C., ended a long

relationship with a co-worker in her department. Almost all their friends and acquaintances were people in Washington whom they'd known as a couple. The woman did not feel comfortable asking the friends she knew socially to start introducing her to eligible men. And on the other hand, she had a very hectic schedule that left little time for her to seek out new people on her own.

Taking the efficient approach, she went to an exclusive (and expensive) matchmaking service. During an extensive interview, she told the agency exactly what she was looking for, describing in detail the income level, interests, and important characteristics of her prospective partner.

Several days later, the service presented her with files and videotapes of several possible candidates. She selected two and arranged to meet both of them. One of the men turned out to be just what she was looking for. Six months later, they were married.

Not for everyone. But if you can afford it, this approach might be right for you.

Whatever approach you decide to take, keep in mind that you *can usually choose* whether you want to play the numbers game—and also choose how you want to play it. It is not unreasonable to speculate that most people can probably meet somewhere near a hundred new people in the next year. Not all those people will even come close to being possible mates, of course. But nonetheless, if you are willing to make the effort to meet a large number of people, you significantly improve your chances of involvement.

Chapter 27

How Can You Nurture a Relationship?

Christine, a thirty-one-year-old illustrator, saw Ray when she was warming up for a run in the park. They caught each other's eye, and she knew he was interested, but it wasn't a situation where she felt comfortable approaching him. Fortunately, she saw him again at a party, and a friend introduced them. After they had talked for a while, Christine asked him whether he would like to meet her for a movie they'd been discussing.

They've been seeing each other ever since:

It's been two months now. Ray has been single for ten years. He was married for eight years. And I have to say that, as far as I'm concerned, I have really thought twice and thought very hard about this person.

I'm curious about his past and I wonder how many people he's been with. I found out maybe five weeks into the relationship that, just before we met, he had ended a relationship with someone he'd been seeing for three years.

I have not been involved with him sexually. For

me, that's usual. I've had five boyfriends in my life and never had a one-night stand. I've always been a little skeptical.

But I think he's kind of hesitating, as well. There might be more reasons than I know, but interestingly, we've really spent a lot of time getting to know each other.

I would say we're uncommitted, but things are moving. I'm thinking about a relationship more and more, and it really is a very healthy part of living.

But the other thing is—and I felt it last night—the vulnerability. I hate that feeling. You're exposing yourself to rejection. It's such a cliché, but so real.

Ray is someone I like very much. That's scary. It's put me in a weird position. He's hit a nerve. There's a risk going on.

Nurturing a Relationship

What happens when you like your single life, but a relationship starts to grow? How can you nurture romance and, at the same time, protect the lifestyle that is yours alone? What are the risks, the costs? What does it feel like to be open and vulnerable and risk all the feelings that go with romantic love?

At a time like this, you can help yourself by knowing that involvement is what you want. *Is* involvement what you want?

In any relationship that is moving toward involvement, you are likely to be frightened at times by what involvement means—dealing with another person's wants, desires, and feelings; discovering more about your own needs; learning about compromise, selfishness, and consideration.

Add to this infatuation, romance, passion, and sexual preferences, and you have a complex arena. In a romantic relationship you are likely to have moments of hopelessness and extreme doubt, but also moments of excitement and exhilaration. In the midst of a romance, if you ask yourself every morning whether or not you want to be in that romance, it is quite possible that every day you will have a different answer.

But if you know that involvement *is* what you want, and that the person is right for you, you can free the energy that it takes to nurture a relationship.

Are You in an Authentic Love Affair?

Some people are capable of altruistic love—that is, love for a higher good or purpose—but I have never seen this in a romantic love affair. You have your own needs that are selfish in the *best* sense. You want your love to be returned; you want the respect and companionship of your partner; and you are looking for a general agreement in your goals together.

At the same time, this doesn't mean that you are grasping everything for yourself and not reinforcing the other person. Romantic relationships are self-reinforcing. You get pleasure out of doing for your partner, so you continue to do it. If you think you are moving toward an authentic love affair, ask yourself these questions:

- Is the other person's self-satisfaction important to me?
- Do I think about the other person's goals?
- Do I want the other person to have satisfying relationships with friends and family, as well as with me?

- Do I want this person to have his or her own interests, even when I don't share them?
- Do I want this person to develop his or her own independence and self-sufficiency along with *our* relationship?

If you can answer "Yes" to these questions, chances are that you are in an authentic love affair, or moving in that direction. While these may seem like altruistic traits, they really aren't, because you are benefiting through the joy that having this kind of attitude toward the other person can trigger. That's what makes it actually selfish! If you want the relationship to continue and you want to be nurtured, it's in your selfish interest to nurture the other person as well.

Of course there are times in any relationship when needs are in conflict, when one or the other requires more room, or when communication isn't what it should be. But if you share a basic desire to work on the relationship when issues arise, then you can usually resolve conflicts as they arise.

Stages of a Relationship

Between the initial meeting with someone who might be a love interest and the eventual commitment to a relationship, there are at least seven steps of development. Each step involves certain transitions, and each poses its own special issues. But the ability to work through these transitions to the next stage of a relationship is an indication that you are, indeed, moving toward commitment.

1. *Initial attraction.* What causes men and women to fall in love? Destiny? Desire? A magical match of minds and hearts?

Falling in love is a chemical reaction. No one under-stands what triggers it (or just what the chemistry is). We merely know that timing has a lot to do with it and that it's there with certain people and not there with others. And when it begins to happen, we certainly do everything in our power to intensify it.

2. *Recognition of the uniqueness of your contact*. A lot of people actually fall in love with love itself. Then, at some point, when the other person's character sur-faces, you become aware of who it is that you've actu-ally fallen in love with and everything changes. That's what we call an ill-fated love affair. The chemistry is there, but the other person really isn't.

If you are really in love with that other person, you come to know your partner's character and appreciate his or her qualities. The uniqueness of your contact appeals to you. The person seems worthwhile and ap-propriate. The specialness of this relationship usually means that you do not feel compelled to seek other romantic contacts to fulfill your needs.

3. *Emotional peaks*. At times, you have an extreme sense of well-being, or chronic pleasure. You know that things are going well. You're in love, and it's recipro-cated and mutual.

But there may also be the valleys—feeling vulnera-ble, risking hurt, wondering whether you may be re-jected. In her relationship with Ray, Christine experi-enced both the emotional highs and lows that characterize this stage.

4. *Reality*. In the early stages of the relationship, you are likely to be spending an increasing amount of time together. It's possible to be suffering from too much togetherness, particularly if you believe that it's necessary to "be one" with the other person. If there is

too much togetherness, then one or both of you may begin to feel cramped or to lose your individuality.

In order for a relationship to work, each person's individuality should be intact to an acceptable degree. Of course, you may be feeling at one with each other when you are making love or being very intimate—and that's great! But don't let that feeling generalize to such an extent that neither one of you can breathe.

In the reality stage, you are reminded that your relationship is only one part of your life. As important a part as it may be, by focusing on it almost exclusively, you could be throwing yourself into a serious state of imbalance.

If the relationship is everything that you idealize it to be, it will not fall apart through the mere act of balancing your life.

5. *Agreement and recognition that a relationship does and will exist.* The first person who tells the other one, "I love you" in a relationship, really pushes up the ante. It often can draw the other person closer. Or it can be the end of the relationship altogether.

When someone tells you, "I love you, but . . . ," no matter what the rest of the sentence is, you are best advised to ignore everything before the "but." Listen only to the end of the sentence. Depending on what comes after, it could be a signal that the other person is not contemplating the kind of commitment that you envision.

6. *Attempts to integrate emotional peaks with reality.* As your relationship moves toward commitment, you have survived at least one or two critical issues. You are now past the stage where initial infatuation has worn off and are confident that this is a long-term relationship.

The loving experience in your relationship depends on three components:

- The intimacy component—feelings of closeness, connectedness, and bondedness that one experiences in a loving relationship
- The passion component—the drives that lead to romance, physical attraction, and sexual consummation
- The decision/commitment component—reaching the decision that you love someone and are committed to maintaining that love in the long term

But all the components of love need to be balanced with reality. Can you maintain intimacy and passion in a continuing relationship? Has the decision that you love each other been reached on both sides—and do you share the commitment to maintain that love? Do you share equally and jointly in making your commitment become a reality? Does your relationship work with your day-to-day lives?

7. *Commitment.* You are willing to relate to the other person at a truly intimate level. But if you have areas of your life that you choose not to share with the other person, it's okay and does not necessarily lessen your commitment.

Open to Opportunity

What is your idea of how you happen to fall in love with somebody? Is it something over which you have no control—or can it be, for you, a conscious decision?

There may have been many people who did *not* approach you in the course of your life because at the time you looked unapproachable. Few people will approach you if you look as though you are going to rebuff them. It is also unlikely that you will meet someone or be approached if you appear desperate.

It's most important to realize that your special person can come along at any moment. Rarely does it happen at the moment you imagine it will.

If you have decided your goal is involvement, you might look in the last place where you would expect to find that person. It could be the first place to start.

Chapter 28

How to Manage a Relationship and Still Be a Good Parent

Lorraine, a thirty-eight-year-old homemaker, has three children—two daughters, aged eight and three, and a son who is five. She was divorced two years ago. About her children and relationships since then, she observes:

> My children provide me with a sense of family that I'd be missing if I didn't have them. They are great kids. But there are times when being a single parent puts you on a short leash when it comes to your social life.
>
> A lot of men who would ordinarily be interested in me immediately write off a long-term relationship. They might want a relationship with me, but not with my children as well.
>
> And when I bring a man back to my house, it's like high school days when my parents were up in the bedroom and we were down on the couch necking. Now it's the children who might peek around the corner and see something they're not supposed to see.
>
> Also, getting a good baby-sitter is very hard. The one I have now is great in every way—except

she is compulsive about the times we agree on. I'm afraid to come home late because I may lose her.

The children's father takes them every other weekend, either for one or one and a half days. But I have them all the rest of the time. So most of the parenting responsibility falls to me.

Single parents do have special issues when they are seeking relationships. Developing a romance or having an overnight guest can be awkward with children at home. And practical obstacles, such as baby-sitters' schedules, can make it difficult to exercise the freedom you would otherwise have.

But often there are ways to handle those factors so that you can have the life you want and still be a loving and responsible parent.

Single-Parent Questions

When you have children to care for, many questions arise which childless singles do not have to consider:

- Do you think potential partners are scared away because you are a parent?
- Are you concerned about making the most of visitation time with your children?
- Do you wonder *when* you should introduce your child to someone you're seeing?
- Do you worry about how to answer a child's questions about your romantic life?
- Are you concerned about the legal consequences of getting involved with someone?

What follows are answers to some common questions that single parents ask—and suggestions of ways to help you resolve some of the dilemmas that arise in single-parent families.

QUESTIONS SINGLE PARENTS ASK MOST OFTEN

1. Are potential partners scared away because I am a parent?

Andrea, who is a thirty-one-year-old journalist, has custody of two children—Brian, who is six, and Jill, three.

> I'm very happy with my work and also with my kids. But I've come to know a certain expression that comes over a man's face when you tell him you have children at home. He may say, "That's wonderful—it must be great to be a mother!" But his eyes sort of glaze. I can't really blame him. Why would a single, unattached male want to get tied down with someone who is already raising two kids?

Several months after her divorce, Andrea became very interested in Peter, a man three years older, who had never been married. The subject never came up, so she did not tell him about her children until the third date.

When Andrea did finally mention her kids, Peter did not seem particularly concerned. They continued to date, and it seemed as if the relationship was growing. In fact, Andrea was almost ready to introduce him to her children when Peter abruptly began seeing another woman and broke off his involvement with Andrea.

Although Peter did not appear to lose interest *immediately* after she told him about her children, Andrea was certain that she scared him away. That experience was painful. In order to avoid being hurt like that again,

Andrea resolved to be very open about her children on the first date.

For Andrea it was important to be aware of the men who might be appropriate partners—and to separate the appropriate ones from those who had very low potential for the relationship she wanted. If he showed an interest in the children (even though he didn't meet them right away), Andrea felt more confident that her having children living with her would not become an issue later on. To her, a man who had children of his own or at least liked children showed the greatest potential.

■ *The Issue: Appropriate partners when you have kids.* If you have a child or children and you are dating people who dislike or have little interest in children, you are probably better off considering these as interim rather than potential permanent relationships that might lead to commitment. By expecting that the person will change, you may be setting yourself up for disappointment later.

As a relationship develops, it eventually becomes important to introduce your significant other to your children. If, over time, there's an irrevocable clash between them, your relationship might not be feasible, no matter how romantic you both feel when you're alone.

2. How do I make the most of visitation time with my children?

Clifford's son, Paul, was one and a half years old when Clifford was divorced. The marriage ended stormily, and Clifford demanded generous visitation as part of the settlement. He knew he wanted to spend time with his child.

Following the divorce, Clifford took care of his son every weekend. In his social commitments, he was very clear about setting aside most of the weekends primarily to be with his son. But he was firm about not wanting visitation time to be just a time to entertain Paul. Clifford wanted to have as much of a relationship with his son as he could, given the limitations of the divorce and the fact that he did not live with Paul in an intact home.

Clifford only dated women who understood and accepted his priorities. If a woman was not willing to acknowledge and participate in the time that he gave to Paul, she was not for him.

■ *The Issue: Balancing time with your kids and socializing.* If you have to balance visitation with your social life, the guiding principle during the time you have together with your child or children is to make your activities and the general climate as normal for all of you as possible. That way, your child will also have much less difficulty adjusting when he or she goes home to the custodial parent. Remember, you have divorced your spouse, not your children!

3. When should I introduce my child to someone I'm seeing?

Nancy, a thirty-nine-year-old single parent, had custody of an eleven-year-old daughter, Kristin. Nancy works part-time as a sales trainer and has an active social life. Some of her relationships have been brief, and she found that she had to decide how much to tell her daughter about her dating activities. Her conclusion:

> A lot of my relationships were very low-key at this point. I would never introduce a man I was dating to Kristin until I was fairly certain that I was serious about him—and the relationship was going somewhere. Otherwise, I think it would be confusing for her.

■ *The Issue: When to introduce someone*. When you are beginning to get more involved, it's time to let the other person meet the kids. Make some observations: How does your friend interact with the kids? Does the adult make an effort to get to know them? Does the person you're seeing seem threatened or jealous of them? Is he or she competing with the kids for attention?

If your partner resents your children's presence, and seems unlikely to change, you could feel quite torn as long as you're in this relationship. Your children are here to stay. The person you're dating might not necessarily be. Any adult who puts a parent in the position of having to choose is exhibiting very immature behavior.

The younger the child, the more likely he or she is to be affected by or become attached to the new person. Introduce that person casually at first. Little by little, your friend and your child can begin to interact.

Remember, your child has experienced a loss and may be hypersensitive about people leaving his life. If the child forms too much of an attachment to someone he thinks will become a permanent part of his or her life, and that person disappears, this can be a lot more problematic for the child than you might have thought. On the other hand, the rule of thumb is that you probably know your children well enough to predict what they can handle. As long as you are sensitive to their cues and the lines of communication are open, there are very few mistakes that are downright irreversible.

Of course, it's not necessarily a disaster if you merely introduce someone to your kids and, later on, the relationship doesn't work out. But if your child or children are introduced to many different partners, they may feel confused and have a hard time letting someone in later.

4. How should I answer my child's questions about my romantic life?

Nancy had to decide how much to tell Kristin about the men she was dating. This became especially important when Nancy began dating Russell. They were beginning to see each other frequently, and the relationship seemed to be moving to a level of greater commitment. Russell wanted to meet Nancy's daughter, so Nancy had him over for dinner.

After Russell left, Kristen asked whether her mother planned to marry Russell.

> All I could tell her was, 'I don't know.' That's the truth. I said I liked him a lot, and down the road marriage might be a possibility. But I also assured Kristin that she could ask me about him, and I would tell her about anything that might affect her. She is very happy in her school, and she's just finding her place in a social group, so that's very important to her right now. I think her main concern is that she might be yanked out of school and end up in a strange place if I suddenly decided to up and marry. I assured her that as of now I have no such plans. She was relieved.

■ *The Issue: Answering children's questions.* Children begin to ask questions about a parent's dating or partners at various ages. Tell them the truth. If you are seriously involved with someone, it's okay to let them know. On the other hand, there is no reason why they need to know the details of your relationship that don't concern them.

Often, they simply and merely want assurance that everything that affects them will be all right. They may fear being told, suddenly, that their whole life is going to change without their needs being considered. They will usually ask what they need to know. If you answer them truthfully, they will usually be sufficiently reassured about the issues that concern them.

5. *What are the legal consequences of getting involved with someone?*

If you are in the midst of a divorce or custody battle, it could be very unwise for you to introduce anyone you're dating to the children or to tell them too much about what's going on in that area of your life. If you think there are legal implications you should be aware of, check first with your lawyer.

SINGLE-PARENT ISSUES

As a single parent myself, I've lived through many of these same concerns. Here are some of the other issues that seem to recur frequently in the lives of single parents:

■ *Issue: Keeping roles straight—without guilt.* Parents sometimes let their children become too tyrannical and set the rules. Often, this is not out of choice but out of guilt.

There is no reason to feel guilty for your divorce or separation. Children from intact, happy homes certainly have the best of all worlds—but your home, with your ex-spouse, was probably not a happy one, since your relationship led to divorce. Research has shown that kids who live in a happy single-parent home have a higher sense of self-esteem than those who come from *un*happy intact homes. So, if you do feel overly guilty for the choices you have made, seek counseling if necessary, but don't act out your guilt toward the kids. If you provide a happy home for your child and keep your role as parent straight, you will be for them as much as any parent can be—single or otherwise.

■ *Issue: Pleasing your children.* It is obviously essential that your children be well taken care of. All but the most irresponsible parents would probably consider that foremost.

But you may be committing the reverse error if you chronically deprive yourself on their behalf. You may be using your children as a smoke screen—that is, using them as an excuse to avoid some of the risks of getting out in the world. Or you might use them as an excuse for not doing other important things that you *would* be doing for yourself "if it were not for the children."

■ *Issue: Dealing with jealousy.* Beware of involvement with someone who expresses too much jealousy over the attention you pay to your kids. It is very possible that an involvement with this person will be a disservice to everyone.

Some jealousy is normal. In fact, you may even become a little jealous if your friend pays more attention to your kids sometimes than he or she pays you. That's resolvable. But where there's a chronic sense of competition that's perpetuated by the adult, consider this a warning sign of things that may come if the involvement deepens.

Your children, on the other hand, usually can be shown that a new person in their life will add more than he or she takes away. If nothing else, it adds to your happiness and thus to your ability to be a parent.

Where Does the Relationship Fit In?

Although many single parents are seeking romantic involvement, each of us must decide for ourselves what kinds of relationships we can handle at this time. Thus, you may have found that romantic attachments are not a priority right now.

If you are a single parent and are looking for involvement, you know how demanding such a lifestyle can be. Knowing that you *can* choose to manage your children and a relationship at the same time gives you the freedom to explore all the possibilities.

Part Five

The Perils of Sex—What Do They Mean to You?

Ten years ago, if I were writing a book about living single, the inevitable chapter on sex might include some information on diseases we knew about that were curable. But primarily, the chapter on sex would discuss issues such as contraception, giving yourself permission to enjoy your body and explore your sexuality, and dealing with the guilt that some people experience when they become liberated from old sexual values and mores.

Ten years ago, we would talk more about what men want—and what women want—early on in a sexual relationship.

We would talk about not allowing yourself to be coerced into sex—the flip side of giving yourself permission to enjoy it.

We would discuss the methods and responsibilities for contraception.

And finally, we would talk about venereal disease. But back then, we were in that period of history between the time when cures for syphilis and gonorrhea were perfected and the time when genital herpes—a new, incurable form of venereal disease—became a source of national concern among sexually active singles.

We were also living in a time when AIDS was unknown.

Chapter 29

Sexually Transmitted Diseases

There are hundreds of diseases that can be transmitted sexually. The most common is gonorrhea, which is the most frequently reported communicable disease in the United States. Other common diseases include syphilis, vaginitis, chlamydial infections, nongonococcal urethritis (NGU), pelvic inflammatory disease (PID) or salpingitis, and Hepatitis B.

It is beyond the scope of this book to address each of these diseases separately. Instead, I would like to concentrate our attention on the issues that are of the utmost concern today.

Those issues are herpes and AIDS.

Herpes

Although herpes now seems far less grave in comparison with AIDS, it often is experienced as being both a physically and emotionally devastating experience. What sets herpes aside from other venereal diseases is the fact that there is no cure for it and that it can be transmitted by an unethical or unwitting sexual partner.

In the early 1980s, when genital herpes began to spread mostly among the upscale single population, we heard people describing themselves as social lepers. For the first time in a while, a one-night stand could be for keeps. No more could megadoses of penicillin pull you immediately out of the woods. (Herpes is caused by a virus, not a bacterium, and unfortunately viruses do not respond to penicillin.)

It was, and still is, impossible to estimate just how many people have herpes, but the range has been placed at somewhere between ten and thirty million. The only remedy is prevention. When outbreaks of herpes became widespread, support groups for herpes sufferers began springing up all over the country, and people who joined these groups felt much less isolated than they had been previously.

For those who knew they had herpes, simple rules that would make sex as safe as possible were developed. Clinical evidence showed that outbreaks could be brought on by stress—quite often (after the initial outbreak), the stress that generated the outbreak was stress about the outbreak itself! In my professional practice I have helped many people come to grips with their fear of contracting herpes and I have also helped some who were infected to deal with the emotional trauma of the condition itself.

The widespread incidence of herpes brought the issue of *safe sex* into focus.

AIDS

In 1981 acquired immune deficiency syndrome, or AIDS, was identified as a fatal disease. In the United States the disease was found first among three high-

﹥ risk groups: male homosexuals; intravenous drug
users, who would often shoot up with contaminated
needles; and Haitians. AIDS is spread by the exchange
of blood products and also is carried through semen.

It took several years for us to realize that we were
dealing with an epidemic, and then additional time
beyond that to realize that the heterosexual community
can be just as vulnerable as the original high-risk
groups. As things now stand, the definitions of safe sex
are becoming narrower and narrower.

It is beyond the scope of this book to discuss all the
ramifications of venereal disease and, most specifically, of AIDS. (There are many good books on the
subject, which reflect the up-to-the-minute knowledge
of this crisis from both a political and medical stand-
point.) But to continue in the spirit of this book, I
would like simply to help you clarify your choices.
Once you understand them and understand what
others are doing, I am confident that you will pick the
options that will work best for you.

A Few Facts

■ Panic never helped anyone—but the flip side of
panic is stupidity. Somewhere between those two extremes is probably the right attitude.

■ The ways in which women have most commonly
become infected have been through intravenous (IV)
drug use (themselves), through sex with IV drug users,
and through sexual contact with bisexual men.

■ If you're relying on the media for the answers,
you will probably get a lot of mixed advice. Many
sensationalistic articles have appeared that were anec-
dotal in nature. Such articles paint a devastating picture of the effects of the disease, but do not give a clear
picture of the extent or the limits of the epidemic. On
the other hand, more responsible journalism can be

relied upon to report genuine breakthroughs either in discovering a cure or prevention for AIDS or in discussing additional risk factors that research has revealed from time to time.

▪ As of this writing, the tests that exist which can screen your blood for the AIDS antibody essentially indicate whether you have been exposed to the virus. However, it can take up to six months for the antibody to be produced in sufficient quantities so that the test can detect it. So someone who shows a negative may be carrying the virus if it was transmitted to that person less than six months before. (That means, if you are tested today, you should also be tested six months from now to confirm that the test is negative. Someone who tests negative but carries the virus can also spread it during that six-month period.) In addition, there are probably other ways, not quite as apparent, that false positives or false negatives can show up in testing.

▪ If AIDS had come along in the fifties, before the sexual revolution, it probably would not have impacted society the way it has now. Indeed, the sexual revolution gave us license, and that license is now making concern about AIDS a factor in many lives.

Changing Sexual Patterns

Since no one can give you a foolproof way to handle the situation in your own life, I'd like to present a number of people who have changed some of their sexual patterns directly as a result of their concern about AIDS. I think the range of viewpoints expressed by these people will help you not only in evaluating your own attitude toward the subject of AIDS but also in observing how widely the assumptions or beliefs of a potential sexual partner may differ from your own.

At one extreme, one can ignore all of the warnings and do things just as in the good old days of not so long ago. At the other extreme, some have chosen total celibacy. Most, I would say, have found their level of comfort somewhere in between. As you consider the choices these people have made, consider too your own. The Attitude Inventory at the end of this chapter will give you the opportunity to survey your personal attitudes and make some decisions about your own sexual behavior.

SCOTT

"I'm more likely to get killed in a car crash than to get AIDS from a woman."

Scott is a thirty-two-year-old investment counselor who lives in Philadelphia. An active heterosexual who has never had a homosexual encounter, he lived with a woman for two years, starting when he was twenty-four years old. Since then, he has dated many different women, and usually expects to sleep with them early in the relationship.

> It's her choice [he says]. *I* know I'm not gay and I don't shoot drugs. I don't hang around prostitutes either.
>
> I can understand why women are worried. I would be too. And if a woman wants me to wear a condom, I will. But I don't feel threatened myself because the odds are so far against a man contracting it from a woman.

Scott does not carry condoms with him and he has never been tested for AIDS. Although he feels that he is in a low-risk group, he continues to scan articles about AIDS to keep informed about medical findings and sex recommendations. With both male and female friends, he sometimes discusses the social and ethical issues—whether tests should be mandatory, whether AIDS carriers should be publicly identified, whether children having AIDS should be allowed in schools, and whether health and social services for patients should be government-run. But he has not met anyone personally who, to his knowledge, has AIDS.

Since the end of his two-year relationship, Scott has not been involved with anyone he says he would seriously consider marrying.

Scott represents a type of man, probably very common today, who believes that it is virtually impossible for heterosexual men to get AIDS. I could not conceive of venturing a guess as to whether, in the long run, he will be safe, because of the very way the AIDS issue has evolved—with one piece of new information surfacing after another. Obviously, Scott represents one extreme in attitude. At this moment it is impossible to predict whether ultimately he will be part of a new high-risk group. I don't endorse Scott's attitude.

HELEN

An attractive, intense professional woman in her late thirties, Helen enjoyed many kinds of sexual activity during the 1970s. When she was in her twenties she had a number of bisexual lovers. She was part of a circle of friends who considered bisexuality an evolution of sexual freedom and respected bisexual males as men who were free of homophobia and could openly express and experience their femininity.

When the realities of the AIDS scare came into the news, Helen went into a depression. Afraid that one of her previous lovers had been a carrier, she was certain that a test would prove positive. In recent months she has not been feeling well, and in reading articles about

AIDS, she realized that some of her symptoms might be signs of the early stages of the disease. Yet she could not bring herself to take the test.

When her depression became more severe, she sought therapy. The main reason she wanted to take the test was that, in case she proved positive, she could at least know where she stood in life—and otherwise feel safe and free. She was very concerned that the test remain confidential. After discussing her options, she decided to take the test after all, at a clinic where those tested remain anonymous.

The test was negative. Released from her anxiety about AIDS, Helen immediately took tests for the other symptoms she was experiencing and found out she was somewhat anemic—a condition that is quite manageable.

After she had taken the test and had begun to have sex again, she found that the scare had made her a proponent of safe sex methods:

> I *know* what precautions I want to take for my own peace of mind. Anyone who cares about my feelings at all will go along with that. And if he *doesn't* care about my feelings, I don't care about having sex with him anyway—so where's the loss?

LUCILLE

Lucille had a brief sexual encounter in 1981 that led to herpes. She was devastated. She had always pictured herself finding the right man and settling into marriage, but she thought herpes would make that impossible. She stopped dating, and she consciously avoided men who seemed to be interested in her. During one severe outbreak, she considered suicide. But there was a hotline number—and she called it.

As a result of that phone call, Lucille joined a herpes support group. One member of the group was someone she recognized from work. She was afraid of being discovered at first, but she soon found out that he and all the other members of the group maintained complete confidentiality. As stress decreased, so did the number and severity of outbreaks. She was relieved to be able to date another member of the group. The usual explanations were unnecessary with him, since they both knew they had herpes. Lucille was relieved that she didn't have to worry about "when to tell him"—or convince him she was okay to be with. He already knew.

Lucille and Rob were married in 1983. Lucille was where she wanted to be, married to a man she found compatible, and herpes was no longer an issue. For unrelated reasons, their marriage ended in divorce several years later. The divorce proceedings were concluded amicably.

Now that Lucille is single again, she is using her experience with herpes in a rather positive way—that is, to accept the inconvenience of safe sex a little more than most people would.

I'm not afraid of AIDS—and I'm not going to be. But I have known for years what it's like to have safe sex. A lot of people don't. They think they're being deprived of their freedom because *now* they have to be careful. They don't realize that if you want to go on with life-as-usual, you have to get used to thinking about your health and taking precautions as an everyday matter. You do it for your own safety and for the sake of the other person.

Lucille believes that AIDS research will produce breakthroughs—a vaccine, reliable treatment, or both. In the meantime, she is now dating again. Because she considers condoms too unreliable, she does not have intercourse or oral sex with the men she dates. Sex is limited to mutual masturbation, usually with extensive foreplay. She openly discusses her concerns about AIDS with men she dates. Lucille says she will not have intercourse until she is ready to marry again and until she and her partner have been tested AIDS-negative. After the first test, she would want her partner to use a condom and a spermicidal jelly until the six-month phase was over and he had been tested again.

> I know the stress that I would feel if there were the slightest risk. It's not good for my health to experience that kind of stress, and it certainly doesn't improve my sex life. Some people think precautions are useless anyway. For me, the *only* sex I can enjoy is when I know I've taken every precaution.

JACQUI

Jacqui was one of the callers on my program one night when the subject was AIDS. Views similar to hers were expressed by a number of listeners that night who called into say that AIDS had made them a lot more cautious.

"I'm terrified by AIDS," Jacqui stated flatly. "It has meant the end of my sex life, and I'm frustrated."

She said if she ever met someone whom she would consider a potential soul mate, she would insist that they take the test together. If the results were negative, she said she would insist that they practice safe sex methods until they were retested and assured that nothing had occurred in the previous six months. After that, she said, she would feel safe in practicing normal sex.

But that's all theoretical [she added]. I'm not even looking for a man right now. I think the situation is very discouraging, and I don't like the way the rules keep changing. First they said it was just gay men and intravenous drug users. Then it turned out that heterosexual contact with non-IV drug users can put you at risk. Now they're saying it can even be carried through saliva—and deep kissing may be dangerous—though I don't think that's been proven. That's why I don't believe *any* kind of sex is safe unless you're both tested. Obviously, I'm not going out of my way to meet great sex partners right now.

Jacqui also said that she didn't relish the thought of remaining celibate, but given the current situation, that was her choice. Ironically, she noted that she had developed more close friendships with men than she ever had before.

STEVE

Another caller on that show, Steve, said he was gay. He'd taken the HIV test, and the results showed he had not been exposed to the AIDS virus. But because of AIDS, Steve has decided to abstain totally from homosexual activity.

Some time before, he said, he'd had a period in his life when he was involved with a woman in a "semi-satisfactory way." Now, he said, he had decided to try to see whether it would be possible for him to enjoy a heterosexual relationship again.

RIVKA

A number of the callers on that program were married. Rivka said that she had been sexually unsatisfied throughout her marriage. She was still in the process of making up her mind whether to get out of her marriage.

Four or five years ago, I would have got out. Now it's beyond that point. I'm not going to start looking for a relationship with this thing [AIDS] going on. I'm not totally happy with my marriage, but I think I would be much more dissatisfied without any sex at all.

Toward the end of the call, she declared that she was going to work on the relationship through counseling. She said she was sure that the choice to stay married was the right thing for her, given the current climate.

MADELINE

There were also a number of callers, both male and female, who raised the question of whether condoms reduced sexual pleasure. Madeline said she keeps condoms by her bed and carries them with her. Some men object, some don't, but since she found out about AIDS, she has never been talked into having intercourse without using a condom.

She commented:

I know some men really do experience a loss of pleasure. Some have a difficult time keeping an erection. But from my point of view, anything is better than going through an interrogation about your sexual history—and then having all kinds of doubts and worries afterwards.

The best medical experts in the country are telling us, 'Use a good condom with spermicides.' I realize there's still a small percentage of risk, but I'll believe the experts. If I go to bed with someone, it's with the understanding that we do everything the way you're supposed to, and we both have the same rules.

Chapter 30

How Do We Talk About AIDS?

For anyone who is having an active sex life—or *wants* one—AIDS is an issue that won't go away. As the examples in the previous chapter show, each person finds his or her own way of dealing with it. But the people who talk to me about their concern with AIDS all have one thing in common: they are willing to deal with it.

But how do we discuss the subject with a prospective sex partner, with an old friend, or with someone to whom we feel romantically attracted?

Gently, but frankly.

If the other person refuses to take the subject seriously, or seems to be evasive, you have every right to be skeptical about that person being an appropriate sex partner. It's true that you may have a higher level of concern than your prospective partner, but that does not mean you should reduce *your* level of concern in order to accommodate someone who does not take this life-and-death issue seriously.

How do you decide what you're going to do—and then do it? What will happen the next time you're seeing someone who might become a sexual partner? How are you going to handle your sexuality if you are a single not in a committed relationship?

One word of caution, and that is to say that the time to make this decision is not while you're sitting on a couch in the heat of passion. The wise will have a very clear view of what they will and won't do when the encounter turns sexual.

The subject needs to be discussed frankly, openly, and in a matter-of-fact manner. This is not an "If you win, I lose" issue. This is clearly a win-win situation, where prudent caution benefits both people. Potential lovers who fail to see that reality are probably worth avoiding.

Some New Ways to Talk About Sex

If you want to discuss safe sex with a potential partner, but you don't know where to begin, here are some general ideas. The words, of course, will be your own. But remember, you *can* push the conversation in the direction you want it to go—and give yourself the opportunity to express your preferences and concerns.

As a general topic . . .

"A lot of my friends are really concerned about AIDS. But everyone seems to have a different opinion about safe sex."

"I saw a news report last night . . ."

"I read in the paper . . ."

"I heard an interview . . ."

"I was astounded to find out . . ." (and simply mention a specific aspect of AIDS)

To explore your potential partner's attitude and experience . . .

"With all the news about AIDS, I've never met anyone who has it—at least that I know about. Have you?"

"Do you think this AIDS thing is overblown?"

To clarify your own position . . .

"I don't believe in taking unnecessary risks with my health."

"It seems as if people are being more careful about sex and relationships. I guess I've developed the same attitude."

"Some people are still gambling by not knowing their partners very well. That doesn't make sense to me."

"I believe a relationship can grow better if there isn't a lot of anxiety up front."

On a more intimate basis . . .

"I *really* enjoyed being with you. I'm just not into taking risks right now. Can we just continue on this basis for a while?"

If you want a sensuous or sexual relationship but do not want sexual intercourse . . .

"I like what's happening, but I'd really like to be careful. So we both don't end up frustrated, let's try _____. What do you think?"

To suggest using a condom . . .

"Everyone's debating whether it's the man's responsibility or the woman's. I'd really like to be with you tonight, so I'll settle the debate and make it *my* responsibility."

"Some day condoms are going to be a relic of the past. At least I hope so. But right now I believe in using them."

"Since you know my views, you know why I think we should use a condom. I know some people don't like to use them, but I think everything will be fine. Anyway, I'm going to try to make it that way."

"Guess who's carrying the number-one pharmaceutical product in America."

To bring up the subject of testing . . .

"I would like our relationship to be a lot freer, but I know we're both thinking of safety. I've decided to take the test. Since I know my own sexual history, I'm pretty certain that the test is going to come up negative. But if I don't get tested, you have to deal with that concern by yourself. So let's settle both of our doubts."

Cautions . . .

There are no words you can say that will help you determine whether someone is a safe partner. A test followed by a six-month waiting period and another test are the only medical means, at this point, to indicate whether you are really safe.

(Perhaps sometime in the future there will be a litmus paper that you can have your partner lick. If it turns red that means stop; yellow means take more tests; and green means "Enjoy sex! Everything is fine!" A nice fantasy, anyway.)

Condoms, when used correctly with the proper spermicide foam, reduce the risk of AIDS. However, all condoms have a percentage of unreliability, and some brands are even less reliable than others.

Unfortunately, the only way you will be safe for certain is to avoid any contact where you will be exchanging bodily fluids. This unquestionably removes a lot of the technique and spontaneity that you enjoy in lovemaking, but it does not exclude stroking, petting, massage, mutual masturbation, and fantasy role-playing.

If you practice fellatio, it is safest if the man wears a condom, and safer if the semen is not swallowed.

With cunnilingus and French kissing the risks are not known. But theoretically you can become infected through mouth sores or other lesions.

What Is Your Choice?

If you think that practicing safe sex is also an exercise in willpower, you're right. The Sexual Revolution told us to listen to our bodies and go with our feelings. Many people became used to that right and to the pleasure that went along with it. It may be very difficult to give up an option that you once had when there is no easy alternative to take its place.

Where do *you* stand in regard to safe-sex practices?

The Attitude Inventory below is an opportunity for you to examine where you stand on making choices for yourself. Record your responses, numbered 1 to 10, in your notebook.

ATTITUDE INVENTORY III
Sex Practices

	YES	NO	
1.	___	___	I believe the risk of AIDS in my group is low enough so that I am willing to take my chances. I do not intend to change my sexual practices unless I know my partner is in a high-risk group.
2.	___	___	I believe that AIDS is a serious potential threat to my health. I intend to abstain from sex until I am in a committed relationship in which we mutually consent to testing.
3.	___	___	I will have sex with any partner as long as we properly use a condom and spermicide.
4.	___	___	I want to abstain from intercourse and oral-genital contact, but I am eager to explore extensive foreplay and mutual masturbation.
5.	___	___	I am not going to have sexual relations until I know that my partner has a sexual history that places him or her in a low-risk group. After that, I intend to have a full sex life with that person.
6.	___	___	I do not intend to have casual sex, but I do expect to have sex with anyone I am seeing on a steady basis.

YES   NO

7. ____ ____   I am comfortable with the sexual
               partner I now have and expect to
               continue practicing sex with that
               person as I have in the past.

8. ____ ____   I am concerned that any current
               partner may be having other sex-
               ual contacts, so I want to change
               our sexual relationship.

9. ____ ____   The whole subject of AIDS fright-
               ens me, and I try not to think
               about it.

10. ____ ____   I would like to implement safe sex
               practices, but I have trouble bring-
               ing up the subject with a prospec-
               tive partner.

EVALUATION: ATTITUDE INVENTORY III

For each YES answer:

1. It is especially important for you to keep well-informed of cautions regarding AIDS. You are leaving a lot to chance.

2. Testing can raise many concerns and issues between partners who are moving toward commitment in a relationship. If you decide to be tested, keep in mind that two tests are required—to be certain—six months apart. Also, if there is any sexual contact outside the relationship between the first test and the second, the results of the second test are not valid.

3.   While condoms are not 100 percent effective, proper use of a condom with an appropriate spermicide has been shown to reduce risk significantly. If this is your preferred option, it is worth your while to find out: (1) which condoms are safest to use; (2) proper use of the condom and spermicide; and (3) ways to use a condom effectively without significantly inhibiting sexual desire or pleasure.

4.   Many kinds of safe sensuous contact can lead to sexual arousal and, depending on the individual, orgasm. Extensive literature is available suggesting ways to heighten anticipation, extend foreplay, and prolong sexual games. Many kinds of erotic stimulation can be enjoyed in a safe-sex mode.

5.   Knowing your partner's sexual history can be reassuring, but keep in mind that you have no way of completely verifying what your partner has told you. Only testing (as explained above) can provide you the reassurance you want.

6.   The reduction or elimination of casual sex certainly reduces risk. However, using sex as an indication of commitment in a relationship can be a double-edged sword. One or both partners may interpret the need for sex as a desire for emotional commitment.

7.   If you have had a long-term sexual relationship with your current partner, continuing to do so is unlikely to increase risk. But this is the case only if your relationship is monogamous.

8.   If your partner's sexual contacts outside the relationship have become a concern, this is something you would want to discuss openly. And you have the right to expect openness from your partner in return. If you feel you are not being taken seriously, or if you have doubts about your partner's level of honesty, you

might want to consider alternative sexual practices or changing your relationship with that person.

9. While AIDS can be a frightening subject, your success in dealing with it depends largely on your ability to act in your own best interest. Keeping yourself informed and introducing self-protective measures that are right for you may be the best ways to overcome your fear and lower your risk.

10. It is understandable that open discussion of your personal health concerns and safe-sex practices may be awkward or seem inappropriate at times. On the other hand, it's likely that sex will be anxiety-producing if you do not practice it in ways that you believe to be safe. Keeping this in mind, make it your assignment to yourself to introduce the subject with your prospective partner. (See above for suggestions on beginning the dialogue.)

Personal Choices

One of the touchiest aspects of this very difficult topic right now is that your personal decisions are influenced by what you read and hear on an almost daily basis. An alarming medical report or news story may cause you to be very fearful—but when you look at the healthy individuals around you, the fear may dissipate and you may wonder whether you have been unduly alarmed. As a result, both behavior and attitudes may be extremely contradictory. One woman expressed this confusion by describing very clearly her own well-informed but ambivalent attitude:

> I know a lot about safe sex, but I don't practice it. Probably because I have a sense of invincibility—that it's not going to happen to me. Which probably isn't true: statistics are showing

that it's happening more to heterosexual women. Still, I know the history and background of people I've had sex with, and I think they're fairly safe.

At the other extreme is the opinion of a woman who began dating again after eight years of a monogamous relationship. She notes with alarm:

I am absolutely astounded at the educated, intelligent men who simply assume, "It's never going to affect me. It has nothing to do with me at all." As soon as I find out they are promiscuous, I just stop seeing them. I think it's shocking.

With so many divergent viewpoints being expressed publicly and privately, it is understandable that making choices for yourself can seem very difficult.

It is my hope that the Attitude Inventory above will help you clarify those choices and realize what behavior is most comfortable for you at this time. And I hope this inventory will heighten your awareness of future information and developments that may influence your choices in the future.

Changing Patterns

Although AIDS may be putting the brakes on many kinds of sexual activity, one positive aspect is that men and women may get to know each other better before they have sex. The result could be that sex will ultimately become more pleasurable. Recently, I heard this comment from a man who had initially been very concerned with AIDS. He told me that his relationships with women had changed significantly since the threat of an epidemic first became news: "There's more flirting and talking, but less pressure to become sexual. The result—more of a friendship. And that's not so bad."

Social patterns for singles *are* definitely changing, and they are likely to continue to change until more is known about AIDS or until the disease is under control. But I have talked to many people who have begun to accept those changes and enjoy them. If sex once again becomes—as it was before the Sexual Revolution—a serious step toward commitment, then it seems likely that courtship is going to resume some of its previous patterns. But if the best of those patterns can be cherished along with the range of knowledge and choices we have gained through the Sexual Revolution, the *new* Sexual Revolution may ultimately bring about changes that benefit both men and women.

Part Six

Survival Strategies

Sometimes we may feel as if we are mismanaging our lives just because one area of concern is giving us trouble.

Christine, a retail store manager, is a single parent with a nine-year-old son, Robbie. Things were going well for her until Robbie began to misbehave in school. She started to receive notes from his teachers and, on several occasions, she got calls from the school counselor. Once, the situation was serious enough that she had to go to school and pick up her son.

Robbie was reluctant to talk about what was bothering him, so her relationship with him became strained. Christine thought his behavior might improve if she was able to spend more time with him, but her job was demanding, and she had trouble rearranging her schedule. Her social life was also suffering because she didn't feel good about leaving Robbie with a sitter. Although Robbie's misbehavior in school was an isolated problem, it seemed to upset everything else in her life as well.

Alex, a thirty-four-year-old service representative for a local manufacturer, enjoys his singles lifestyle, but he has reached a stage of his life where he thinks he would be more comfortable if he had a long-range investment plan and some concrete goals for retirement. But even though this is an issue, he isn't really sure where to begin.

Brenda, a twenty-seven-year-old travel agent, had become very concerned about the city neighborhood in which she was living. In recent months, a single woman had been robbed on the street and one apartment had been burglarized. Brenda had begun feeling insecure in her own apartment—and that feeling made her much less happy with single life than she had been before.

Areas of Responsibility

As single people, we have many areas of responsibility that we must handle by ourselves. A single parent like Christine has all the responsibilities of childcare, schooling, and providing a good home and nurturing environment for the child.

At some point, each of us has some financial concerns that resemble Alex's. Whatever our present means, we must think about our financial security, preparing for emergencies, health care, and retirement.

Like Brenda, we also have responsibilities to ourselves—to make sure we feel secure in our home and our neighborhood.

And of course, there are many other areas of responsibility beyond these. We must decide for ourselves where we choose to live, how we balance our time between "work" and "play," how we take care of medical concerns and security needs, and how we plan for the future.

Survival Strategies

To handle these responsibilities, we need Survival Strategies to help us deal with the *practical* issues in our lives. If you are single, you need to rely more on your own resources and ingenuity to deal with these issues. Other people can help you. But the only one on whom you can rely all the time is yourself!

Of course, we don't *have* to be competent in all areas (though I suspect that most of us—secretly or not so secretly—want to be). But we do have to give some thought to each of the areas that may cause us some concern.

In the case of Christine, her Survival Strategy was changing her job schedule so she did not have to work on weekends. By leaving her weekends open, she found more time to talk to Robbie and to arrange activities for him. Eventually she discovered some of the reasons he was unhappy at school, and she took measures to help him cope with the issues that were troubling him.

Alex's Survival Strategy was to read a basic book about financial planning and to meet with an accountant. Handling his insurance needs and coming up with an investment plan was not as difficult as he had imagined. Once he looked at the financial issues and resolved them, he felt a lot more secure.

Brenda's Survival Strategy was to form a committee in her neighborhood to hire a block guard. (After talking to her neighbors, she found out that many of them were just as concerned about the situation as she was.) Brenda also decided to buy a well-trained dog—and she discovered she not only felt more secure, she also enjoyed the companionship of having a pet at home.

Custom-Design Your Strategies

In addition to some of the guidelines that I'll be giving you in this section, there are books, counselors, and well-informed friends who can help you develop your special strategies.

Here are some of the issues that we'll deal with in the chapters that follow:

- Taking care of people who depend on you
- Medical Concerns
- Planning
- Balancing work and play
- Housing
- Security
- Finances

We hope these chapters raise some issues that you may have been neglecting. For instance:

Taking care of people who depend on you: Do you need help in negotiating conflicting demands that strain your time and energy?

Medical concerns: Did you ever have a health scare that resulted in your feeling helpless because nobody was around?

Planning: Are you putting aside the question of long-term objectives . . . because you're waiting for someone else to come into your life and help you decide your goals?

Balancing work and play: Do you sometimes get so consumed by work that you lose perspective on your nonwork life?

Housing: Do you need some guidance in deciding

whether to move or to buy a house, a co-op, or a condo?

Security: Do you worry about your physical safety because you live alone?

Finances: Are you under-insured? Have you put off providing for emergencies—and for retirement?

Helping Yourself to Achieve Your Goals

If you answer "Yes" to any of these questions, then you will want to go right to the Survival Strategies in this section that correspond with these concerns. Success in one area can quickly lead to success in others.

Continue to jot down useful ideas in your notebook. Then come up with a plan and put it into action!

Chapter 31

Taking Care of People Who Depend on You

If you are a single person with family responsibilities, negotiation is a large portion of the art of living single. If you have children, you are constantly trading off your needs and theirs. You want them to have opportunities and advantages, but you can't totally neglect yourself. Where do you draw the line?

Living with parents can be even more difficult than living with young children. Lois, a woman who went back to live with her parents after her marriage broke up, said, "They began treating me exactly as they did before I was married. I could have been sixteen years old and in high school again. It felt like a total loss of seniority."

Clinton has custody of his two children and lives with his parents. "It solves the baby-sitting problem," he says, "but not much else. My parents act as if they have *three* children—their two grandchildren . . . and *me*. Sometimes I think there are more rules for me than for the two kids."

But there are many people who live with their parents by choice. "It gives me more of a feeling of family than I get living by myself," says Tricia. Now thirty-three, she moved in with her parents four years ago. "There are many things that I choose not to discuss with them," she says. "But as long as we all stick to our own boundaries, I find it much preferable to living alone."

Negotiate

Whether you are sharing your life with children or with parents, the most powerful strategy at your command is *negotiation*. Let the people around you know what your needs are. You have to listen with genuine interest and understanding to find out about their needs, too. And then, negotiate a situation where everybody wins.

Scheduling

You can also make progress here by negotiating. No matter how inflexible the other person seems at first (such as a stubborn teenager who *takes a position* and will not budge), you can succeed if you can show that there will be some benefits on all sides.

Make your schedule *explicit*. Write it down and post it for the following reasons:

■ It lets other people in your household know what you intend to do. They can build their plans around yours, or make arrangements on their own.

■ It sets a precedent: if you're telling them *your* plans, then you have more of a right to expect to know *theirs* (within reason, of course).

■ It gives everyone a chance to negotiate *before the fact*. How many arguments have begun, "Why didn't you tell me . . . ?" By discussing your schedule beforehand, you don't hash over postmortems. You can talk about a night out or a night off *before* it happens. If anyone has a problem, discuss it.

■ It makes things more convenient and increases the likelihood that you'll stay on top of what's going on in your house. If you're working full time and are caught up in other activities, you can sometimes lose track of what your own children are doing. If *your* schedule interferes with *theirs*, be assured you'll hear about it immediately.

If you negotiate *before* the schedule is cast in stone, you still have a chance to be flexible and to avoid a lot of problems. Bargaining is very important when it comes to getting the people who depend on you to give you time to yourself. You need breaks. Get the time you need before you become overstretched, exhausted, and worn down.

That depends on several things:

■ Is time off *possible* right now? Can you get an evening? A quiet hour in the afternoon? A half-hour at noontime? Look for possible breaks in the day when you can find time to shut off your engine and just . . . rest.

■ Can you drop a nonnecessity? If you can't find a gap anywhere, you might want to reevaluate what's going on in your day. What would happen if you *didn't* show up for a meeting? What if the kids had to get their *own* breakfast? What can you drop from your schedule, at least temporarily, without causing undue pain or aggravation?

■ Can someone help you? Sometimes, excessive activity leads to reduced efficiency, because you're trying to do everything yourself. If you're taxiing children around, who can help drive? If you're cooking 90 percent of the meals, who can help reduce that down to 50 percent? If an aging parent is making full-time demands on you, is there someone else who can help you meet those demands?

Consider the possibility of calling upon neighbors, friends, or other family members. You may have more resources than you think, but you'll never know unless you ask.

■ Can you pay for a helper? If you are economy-conscious, you may have difficulty justifying paying for help just so you can have time free. But sometimes it's quite necessary. Time to relax without responsibilities is crucial to the overburdened single. If you can get a sitter or housekeeper for an hour or two, you could be saving more than you realize in health and energy—despite the expense.

Post your breaks as part of your weekly schedule. When you have that time to yourself, protect it like a jewel. Lie in bed and read. Go for a walk. Listen to music. Everyone's needs for quantity and quality free time are different. Know yours and make sure you take it in a way that nourishes you. For a busy person with huge demands, this is *necessary* time for your health and your self.

Steady Help

Steady help, especially live-in help, may seem like a luxury that few people can afford. But if you are one of those who possibly *can* afford it, you could be making a very positive change in your life. Finding the right person can be a long and sometimes difficult process—followed by a period of adjustment for everyone in your household. You can make this a positive move for everyone if you:

- Communicate your reasons for wanting help
- Include your child, children, and/or parents in the decision to hire this person
- Let them talk to the person you want to hire
- Let everyone in your household know the benefits of hiring someone to help you
- Follow through in delivering those benefits.

By having help you get to spend more time with others in your household. When children get home from school, they know someone always will be there for them. If the person you hire cooks meals or taxis kids, you're *all* better off: everyone gets to do more things they'd *like* to do, without the hassles of coordinating schedules.

Having someone else at home also gives you more time for your job (extra hours, extra projects, new challenges), time for yourself (exercise, socializing), and time for the people you care about (children, parents, and friends).

Life with Children

Perhaps you have children, but they are not living with you. Noncustodial parents have special issues and concerns. Even if you just see your children on weekends, it's possible to know them at least as well as the parent who lives with them full time. In fact, a number of divorced men have said to me that they got to know their children better as divorced fathers than they would have if the marriage had stayed together.

Because visitation time is usually time well spent doing things with your child, you may really look forward to your children visiting. It may also be a challenge. Both men and women today are noncustodial parents. Had this book been written one or two decades ago, this section would have been aimed exclusively at men.

Needless to say, your dating life and social life may be affected. (See Part Four, "Getting Involved and Nurturing a Relationship.") But even if you're not romantically involved with someone, a visiting child can be a major disruption and/or preoccupation (as well as a joy) on a weekend.

Here are some considerations to keep in mind when children visit:

- Be consistent. This is most important! When you make plans for a weekend, do everything in your power to avoid changing those plans. If you *must* change plans, explain the reasons to the child. Set up another date immediately and keep that appointment! An unreliable or inconsistent parent can make a child's life very painful. Practically nothing can make him or her feel more unloved.

- Help the child adjust. For the most part, children take approximately a year to adjust to divorce. During that time, some act out in aggressive ways with their parents, friends, and siblings. Others may clam up and become depressed. Be patient. Listen for clues to what may be troubling the child. If he or she is old enough, be open with the child and answer questions as honestly as possible. Of course, that doesn't mean you have to get into all the details of the divorce. Use common sense, and tell the children only what they can understand and need to know.

Patience is the key. Immediately after a divorce is not the time to institute new disciplinary measures or to make any new demands on your child (such as improved performance in school). Make yourself available to your child and put your own pain aside when you're with him or her. Remember, you will heal and so will your children if you are there for them.

- Don't bad-mouth your ex! It is extremely important that *neither* parent poison his or her child's mind against the other parent. This confuses children terribly and may eventually turn the child *against* the bad-mouthing parent. If your parents, friends, or relatives harbor ill will toward your ex, make sure they never express those bad feelings in front of the child. If they don't honor your request, keep them away from your children. A child should maintain a relationship with both parents, unless, of course, there is an extraordinary problem with abuse or molestation.

- Create a relaxed climate when the children visit. You may have heard the term "Disneyland Daddy." The stereotype is a father who takes his children only to the fun spots. They visit the park, the zoo, the science museum—or any other attractions he can think of—just so they have something to do when they visit. Needless to say, there are also "Disneyland Mommies."

To avoid being a Disneyland Parent, make your children as much a part of your new life as possible. When they visit, be appropriate, of course, but carry on many of your normal activities. You'll find that the climate will become a lot more relaxed, and visitation will seem less like a chore. If you only take your children to fun places, you're not giving them a realistic view of you. You're not letting them fit into your life. And, in addition, they will often find it harder to readjust when they go home to their custodial parent.

- Assure your child or children that it's *not their fault*. Children between the ages of four and six have the most difficult time with divorce. They often internalize the blame for the divorce—especially if they overheard their own names in a dispute. Spare nothing in alleviating this unnecessary guilt. Marriages end because they run their course. If the fault lies anywhere, it is in the parents' inability to deal with issues in the marriage.

▪ If your ex is uncooperative, do not use your child as a weapon. If you talk to people who have had some of the bloodiest divorces, you will find that those who have completely recovered can laugh about what happened when full-scale war was raging. Not so the children who have been used as pawns in these battles. They often suffer scars for life and hold deep resentment against one or both parents. In fact, many feel a particular resentment toward the parent who felt he or she was going to turn the child against the *other* parent. Never use your child as a pawn.

Parents and Children

Some single parents have to look after their own parents as well as children.

Fran's daughter was three years old when her parents moved from out of state into her house. Fran's father had been sick for a number of years, and her mother found it too difficult to care for him and care for their house by herself. Fran had a large house, so it was easy for them to stay there.

After her father died, however, Fran realized that her mother would remain as a permanent resident. She was lonely and grieving the death of her husband. Fran could not even think of moving her elsewhere.

At first, Fran felt as if she were now taking care of two children. With some encouragement from other members in her divorce group, however, she began to turn the situation around. She eased her mother into taking more responsibility in running the family and household. Fran's mother became more responsible as a baby-sitter, which freed Fran to do other things. Far from being "another child," her mother gradually became a tremendous help to her, and gained more self-esteem as she felt vitally needed and loved for her contributions to everyone's well-being.

Seeking Help

If you are in a family situation that is increasingly stressful, you may be able to get help and encouragement from groups for single parents. Other members of the group can throw some light on what you're experiencing. Often the tensions in single-parent households are similar, and you can find some common solutions to common problems. Short-term professional therapy also can be helpful in working out some conflict resolutions.

Chapter 32

Medical Concerns

One fear that many of us share is the fear of getting sick when no one's around. If you have to stay home with a head cold for a day or two, that's certainly endurable. But what about those days when you feel *really* sick—you have fever, chills, an upset stomach, or the flu—and there's no one to help you?

Julie, a thirty-five-year-old personnel supervisor, had a bout with mononucleosis that had an emotional as well as physical effect.

"I felt so *powerless,*" she told me. "I was tired all the time. I tried to go back to work, but I was so exhausted I had to leave early. So on top of feeling terrible, I started to worry about my job—and wonder what would happen if I *really* couldn't go back to work for a long time. In fact, it hung on so long, I began to think it might be something *worse* than mono. And that scared me."

As Julie's health improved, so did her outlook. But she didn't forget that feeling of helplessness. When she was well again, she got in touch with a few close friends (one was a next-door neighbor) and asked whether they would agree to be "on-call" for her if she were seriously ill or facing an emergency.

All three agreed. In fact, Julie's neighbor—who was also single—was glad to be asked. She asked if Julie would be "on-call" in return, and of course Julie said yes at once.

Being Ready

For most of us, the bouts of really serious illness are rare. We can prepare for emergencies by having the number of a doctor or ambulance by the phone. If we had an accident, we would automatically get in touch with a number of people—relatives, close friends, or anyone else in our support group.

More often, the illness is minor, but we may feel so awful at the time that the fact of being alone just makes the symptoms seem worse. "I-felt like no one cared," is how many single people talk about being alone and sick.

We don't necessarily need a great deal of medical attention. We'd just like someone to stop by with a bunch of magazines and a bottle of fresh orange juice to see how we are. Wouldn't it be nice to have someone fluff up the pillows and fix chicken soup? *Missing* a person like that can make us feel worse than we really are.

There may be many people who would be very willing to help you out in these ways if you only ask. In fact, they would probably be pleased to be asked. And you don't have to be in dire straits before you request help The first morning you're in bed, call a friend. Even if you think you might be up and about the next morning, just let your friend know that you *could* be cooped up for a few days.

And it's all right to ask your friend if he or she would stop by after work and bring you a few groceries, medicine, or a newspaper. If you're hesitant about doing this, turn the situation around and ask yourself: "Would I be happy to help this friend if she [or he] were sick?"

If the answer is "Yes," don't hesitate to call. You *do* need some support. But be sure to let your friend know that you want to reciprocate if that person is ever in a similar situation.

On-Call Friends

Like Julie, you might want to set up an "emergency network" of three close friends, neighbors, or relatives who are willing to be on call. Keep their numbers by your phone, in case you need to ring them suddenly. By having *three* numbers, you're almost assured that at least one of them will be reachable if you ever need to call.

Also carry these numbers with you. In the unlikely event that you were in a serious accident or found unconscious, the hospital would first call your home. Since there may not be anyone home, that doesn't help you. But if you have the other names and numbers with you, clearly labeled "IN CASE OF EMERGENCY, CALL . . .," the hospital will get in touch with people who really can be there for you.

For Emergencies

In addition, there are a few basic precautions that anyone living alone should consider, just to be on the safe side:

- Keep medical records and insurance information where you can find them quickly. If you have recently come out of a relationship or marriage where the other person kept track of such things, make sure your insurance is up to date and the forms are handy.
- If you *do* have to go to the hospital, does someone have the key to your house or apartment? You might need to have things brought to you, or have someone take care of pets while you're away.
- Keep emergency numbers by your telephone. If you have preprogrammed dialing, program the numbers for doctor, ambulance (or emergency room), police, and on-call friends.

Your Medical Ally

For the single person, your personal physician is your greatest ally. If possible, see one doctor on a regular basis. Be sure he or she is up to date on your medical history, and be sure to share with your physician any special concerns you have about living alone. If you have a chronic condition, allergies to certain drugs, or need for a certain medication, your physician should have some suggestions about medical tags, warnings, or other information you should carry with you.

Although doctors recommend the annual checkup for everyone, it's especially important if you're single, because it's a chance to remind your doctor that you're a patient. A physician who sees you annually is much easier to call on than someone who hasn't seen you in a long time—and that physician will be much better informed.

You can also ask if your doctor will make house calls. Some doctors still do—and if you're living alone it can be very reassuring to know that a doctor *will* come if it's really necessary.

Chapter 33

Planning

Imagine that someone you respect a great deal—parent, teacher, counselor, friend—is sitting across from you at the table. Suddenly, that person asks you, "Where do you see yourself next year?" You answer, and the person then asks: "Well, what about five years from now?" And finally: "What about *ten* years from now?"

This is an unlikely scenario, of course. People don't often sit us down and ask about our long-term plans. When you're living single, you don't even have someone who asks you what you're doing *tomorrow*. It's all up to you! So it may be hard for you to say, "Okay, here's where I want to be five or ten years from now."

But even though it may be difficult, you need to plan ahead.

Making Decisions

One client of mine, Craig, had graduated from Cornell as a history major. Ever since college, he had thought he would return to academic life at some point and get his Ph.D. But, at twenty-eight, he was earning a good salary as a manager for a computer company.

Craig had recently broken off his relationship with a woman he'd been seeing for three years. He was now living alone.

"I used to talk about my plans with her," he said. "But about six months after we broke up, I realized that I wasn't telling *anyone* what my plans were—not even myself. Obviously, no one was going to make any decisions for me. I said to myself: 'I'm single, I have some money in the bank, and no commitments. If I'm going to get started on my Ph.D., now is the time.'"

Craig signed up for his GRE's, got his recommendations together, interviewed at a number of graduate schools, and talked to friends who had gone for their Ph.D.'s. In the end, however, he decided not to apply.

Making that decision taught him something about his goals.

"I realized I had changed. I can't bury myself in the history books again. I do like business—I want to stay in it."

For Craig, taking some action helped him to clarify his goals. And he realized his decisions about what he wanted to do weren't contingent upon making plans with another person in his life. His plans were contingent upon what *he* wanted to do.

Your Goals

For single people, there's often another block to goal-setting, as well. If you expect to get into a relationship or get married within the next few years, you may have the attitude that a lot of things are going to change when you meet the other person. Or if you're seeing someone who might become a mate, you may be deferring your plans until that relationship is clarified.

You put off planning a life *alone* because you're think-ing about *life with someone else*.

But thinking that there *might be* someone in your future usually has the effect of deferring your plans, rather than clarifying them.

Goal-Setting on Your Own

I often recommend to single clients that they try to plan their long-term goals *under the assumption that they're not going to find a relationship.*

If you do get into a relationship, of course, you can always find a way to include the other person in your plans for the future. But I urge you to take the attitude that you're setting your *own* goals for *yourself.* Assume that you're going to live your life on your own—and focus on what *you* want to achieve.

Write It Down

Committing yourself to your goals really requires two steps: writing them down, and telling other people about them.

When you write out your objectives, you help your-self see whether those goals are realistic and achiev-able. Also, if you put them in writing, you can check yourself later to find out how far you've moved toward them.

In your notebook, make a list down the left-hand side of a page:

TODAY _____

THIS WEEK _____

NEXT MONTH _____

NEXT YEAR _____

FIVE YEARS _____

TWENTY YEARS _____

LIFE _____

Across the top of the page, list the parts of your life that are important to you and require goal-setting. CAREER would be one of those columns. But you might also list family, sports, recreation, community involvement, volunteer work, hobbies, or any other topic that is especially important to you.

Now fill in the blanks. You may find that you want to start with writing in the long-term goals (ten or twenty years away), then work backward toward one-day and one-week goals. Of course, you may not be able to fill in *all* the blanks. But don't give up too soon! Consider this a mini-roadmap that will help remind you where you want to go—and when.

The second step is to *tell people*. If you were married or in a relationship before, you probably told the other person what you planned to do. Whether or not another person helps your plan become a reality, the act of talking about it takes you a step farther toward commitment.

For single people, it's important to reach out and tell our friends about our plans, so we *make that commitment* to moving ahead. And talking about your plans also gives your friends and support group the opportunity to share their ideas, assistance, and advice.

Later on, your friends will probably remind you of your goals. A few weeks from now, a friend might ask, "How are your plans for _____ coming along?" That's an incentive to keep you on track.

Meanwhile, be genuinely interested in your friends' goals and be alert to ways in which you can help *them*. If someone is heading back to school, exploring a new avocation, expanding his or her social life, or financing a new venture, you can assist in numerous ways—by providing information or arranging contact with the right people. One of the greatest pleasures is seeing a good friend achieve something that he or she has really wanted for a long time!

Keeping a Mentor

Stay in touch with people who have taken a special interest in your career or your growth and are willing to offer help and guidance. Such a person can be much more objective than your friends or parents. That mentor can be a wonderful guide if you are living single and have to make critical life choices on your own.

Valerie, a thirty-five-year-old training director, told me about a former boss, now retired, who had helped her with a number of choices in her life. He is very active in community affairs, and Valerie says she usually has to call him to make an appointment. But he's always glad to hear from her, and whenever she calls (about twice a year), they arrange to have lunch.

"He listens and asks questions," says Valerie. "I don't think he's ever given me direct advice, but somehow I always come away with a clearer view of what I'm doing and what choices I feel I should be making for myself."

If you have someone who can *listen*, you have a wonderful resource! A true mentor will question your objectives, challenge you, and help you explore new opportunities.

Above all, that person can help you *spell out* your goals so they become clearer to you.

The Relationship Question

But what if a lot of your goal-setting brings you back to the theme: "I expect to find a relationship."

If that's the case, *finding a relationship* is, itself, a very important goal for you—and you will want to refer to the strategies in Part Three ("Romantic Strategies") and Part Four ("Getting Involved and Nurturing a Relationship").

But also keep in mind that the other goals in your single life can be controlled by *you*. Romance and relationships often depend on other people. So the romance-and-relationship goal is much less controllable than your other objectives.

Don't *put off* your life until you find a relationship! If finding a mate is a goal, move ahead with your other plans while you're pursuing that goal as well.

Chapter 34

Balancing Work and Play

"I think I'm becoming a workaholic," Sandra told me. A market researcher for a multinational firm, Sandra has risen fast in the company and she loves her job. But she is concerned that work may be pushing aside too many other things. "I work ten-hour days, I bring paperwork home. More and more weekends, I'm just working and not going out very much. Sometimes I wish someone would just barge into the study and say, 'Hey, it's time to knock it off! Let's go to a movie.'"

Sandra lived for three years with Roger, and the scene she described was fairly typical when they lived together. Usually, he was the one who planned things outside of work. He would call her at the office to ask whether she wanted to go to a movie or out to dinner that night. At home, he was usually the one who suggested things to do on the spur of the moment.

At first, after she and Roger separated, Sandra enjoyed having the extra hours for work. But she had got out of the habit of doing things spontaneously.

"The work part comes naturally," she said. "But I realize I counted on him to balance things out a little. I'm not so good at doing that for myself."

The Balance

Many single people find themselves in Sandra's position if they've been in a relationship where work and play were negotiated between partners. You may come to rely on the other person to interrupt or to suggest ideas for getting out and doing things. When that person isn't there, it's up to you to balance work and play.

Also, for some single people, work begins to take the place of a relationship. In a way, it's *easier* to become a workaholic, because no one's pulling you away and saying, "Hey, take a break!" or, for that matter, "Hey, pay some attention to *me*!"

Many of us are in jobs where there's always more work to do if we want to take it on—and often that work brings external and internal rewards that we need. So we just say "Yes" to a lot of things. And of course, that's fine, if it continues to be rewarding.

But if you want more *play* and you're not getting it, you really have to become your own organizer for a minute. Play time doesn't flow automatically. You might have to put more conscious effort into organizing your play time—separating it from your work time—and figuring out the balance that's best for you.

Here are some ideas on how to make that happen:

■ Plan for yourself, instead of waiting for other people to plan for you—as you may have successfully done in the past. Think about the interruptions and distractions that you may have enjoyed when you were in a relationship. You can enjoy those same distractions on your own, but you have to set them up for yourself.

When you get that impulse to do something on the spur of the moment, why not do it? It could be a great idea—and your chance to take a break! Maybe you have an internal alarm that reminds you, "Go play!"

- Give yourself a reward for work well done. "I study all the time," Claudia told me when she started her graduate work in psychology. "I don't really care about anything else right now. This is a big opportunity and it's important to me."

A year later, though, her pattern had changed. "I've set up my rewards," she told me. "I always plan something for weekends to reward me for doing a great job during the week." It can be as simple as that.

- If your work becomes an energy-draining enterprise that doesn't leave you time for fun and enjoyment, perhaps you can get more support from within your organization and delegate more responsibilities.

Making yourself take some breaks could be good for your professional life as well as your leisure life. We all need interludes to recharge our batteries. Some people find that their best ideas occur to them during relaxed moments rather than when they are working feverishly.

- Combine business and pleasure. "I work with people I enjoy," observes the production coordinator for an independent film company. "I see a lot of people from work on weekends. We have a great time. Where does work end and socializing begin? I don't know! And that's the way I like it."

Finding the Rewards

But what if you can't seem to find the right balance? Blaine holds a middle-management position at a Fortune 500 company. "Something has been dawning on me," he observed. "I've been working very hard for the past twenty years. I make good money. I've earned a lot of respect from the people I work with. But I really don't like my job that much. I don't feel like changing right now—but on the other hand, why am I killing myself, putting all my energy into it?"

Blaine was searching for a way to feel less burnt out, but there were no simple answers. Up to this point in his life, his career had obviously played a very important role in determining his sense of self-reward and satisfaction. He had put a lot of energy into his career, and for many years it provided the returns he wanted. Was the feeling of burn-out temporary—or did it mean that he needed more in his personal life to put his job in a different perspective? Blaine wasn't sure—but he knew he was in pain, and that pain was telling him that something needed to be changed.

Rather than quit his job or take other drastic measures, Blaine took a first step of cutting back his hours and using some overdue vacation time to consider his priorities. Over time, he realized that he had been shortchanging his personal life, but this went along with a recognition that improvements in that area would not automatically make him feel better about his job. He began looking at a career change, possibly two or three years down the road.

As he began to explore some of the avenues toward his new career, Blaine began to meet a new group of people whom he found stimulating and exciting. His job began to seem less restrictive as he began to see his current experience in the light of future career goals.

Blaine realized that his personal and professional life had blended well in the past, as long as his career goals were well defined. By redefining what he wanted to accomplish, he helped himself move away from the "burn-out" cycle. He decided that it was not overwork that was causing him pain, but the feeling that his work was less meaningful than it had seemed before. The more comfortable he felt about his eventual career change, the more his personal life seemed to improve.

For Blaine, it was not a matter of "balancing" work and play as much as blending his personal life with professional goals that continued to be meaningful.

When Does Work Have the Upper Hand?

Many single people find that the amount they work, and the return-on-investment that they get from work, may be directly related to what's happening with other parts of their lives.

You can help yourself by identifying, as well as possible, what you really hope to get from your work. Work *can't* substitute for a relationship or patch up a romance. Nor can it substitute for avocational interests that may bring you great personal rewards—or for a social life that you would like to have. When you are a single person, there's a tendency to plunge deeper into work when you might be wishing for some nurturing or enrichment from other parts of your life. But it's important to identify the rewards you really want, so you can look for them in the appropriate places.

Where Are Your Rewards?

To help you assess what's important to you, look back over the past few years. In your notebook, write WORK at the top of one page and PLAY at the top of the facing page. Then, on each page, respond to the six questions in this Attitude Inventory.

WORK/PLAY ATTITUDE INVENTORY

1. What have been your biggest rewards over the past five years? Ten years?
2. What was the challenge you enjoyed the most?
3. What would you like to see happen again?

4. What do you want to add to your regular schedule?
5. Where did you meet the people whom you enjoy the most?
6. Where did you meet the people who have had the most positive influence on you?

Getting the Mix That's Right for You

Review the Work/Play Attitude Inventory. Were you being the architect of your life, or is there something that you let slide by?

Do your personal goals in any way match the real opportunities of your current employment?

If not, take some time out for a reassessment. How *can* you reach the goals that are most important to you? Does your situation require a career change—a change of employer—or a different balance of priorities?

When you have identified the changes that need to be made to enrich your life, list the steps that you must take to reach your goals. If you divide these steps into "Long-Term," "Shorter-Term," and "Immediate," you can begin to take managable steps. Challenge yourself to stay on top of your goals and timetable for reaching them.

Chapter 35

Housing

Sarah, a thirty-eight-year-old executive secretary, had always assumed she would move into a house as soon as she was married. She had been living in the same apartment for seven years, and she wanted to make a lot of improvements—but working on improvements didn't seem worthwhile as long as she was only renting.

However, Sarah had built up some savings. And after looking at a number of other rental situations, she began to consider the possibility of buying her own home.

Finally, that's what she did:

> It was a big move for me. I finally felt like an adult. I also got out of that pattern of thinking I had to be married before I could make an investment in a home. As soon as I moved in, I began to improve the house, and things kind of fell into place for me. I'm not waiting for someone to come along and give me a permanent home. I'm doing it for myself, and I feel good about that.

Sarah discovered that owning her own house not only gave her a great deal of enjoyment, it also made her feel better about her own outlook and more secure about her future, and about entertaining and enlarging her circle of friends.

What Are Your Options?

If you enjoy your lifestyle and you *like* where you're living, of course there is no reason to change. But if something about your current living environment is making you unhappy, why not look at some other options? Consider these questions:

If you are living by yourself . . .

- Do you want to consider a housemate or co-renter?

If you are renting . . .

- Is it time to buy? (And, if so, a house, a co-op apartment, or a condominium?)

If you own your house or apartment . . .

- Do you want to "buy up" (move to a larger or more luxurious place)?
- Do you want to improve your present residence?
- Do you need to reduce your living expenses for some reason?

Now consider some ways you might want to improve your living condition? Would you like to . . .

- Redecorate?
- Buy new furniture?
- Renovate some areas of your home?

- Make your living areas more comfortable?
- Refurnish? (Which rooms?)
- Add amenities? (Jacuzzi? Workout equipment? New sound or video system?)
- Make outdoor improvements? (Garden? Patio? Pool? Porch garden? Landscaping?)
- Make additions?

Finally, consider your neighborhood:

- Do you feel safe?
- Do you fit in with your neighbors?
- Are shopping areas and other facilities you consider important convenient to you?
- Do you have the parking and/or public transportation that you need?
- Are you living in the neighborhood where you want to be?

These questions are designed to help you consider whether you should make some changes that will improve the quality of your life.

Going Beyond Temporary

One of my colleagues observed that many single people feel as if their homes are temporary. That "temporary" feeling is expressed in their surroundings. They might have no pictures on the walls or no curtains. They may have all their old college furniture. They're not really moved into their lives. *Everything about the place says "temporary."*

Are there signs that you haven't really moved in yet? If so, maybe it's time to buy the new sofa, hang pictures on the wall, or install the wonderful sound system you've always wanted! You know what your financial resources are, so obviously observe their limitations.

But if you're holding back because you fear developing a more permanent lifestyle, chances are there is a lot of unhappiness behind that fear.

Strategies for Fixing up an Apartment

Does your apartment need a new look? Here are several approaches you can take:

- *Do it yourself.* "When I first saw my apartment, I had great plans," Joe told me. "I decided where everything would go. But two days after I moved in, there was a crisis at work—everything caught up with me. Months went by. One day I looked around and said, 'Whatever happened to my great plans?' It was all in my head—I *knew* what furnishings I wanted to buy and I knew how I wanted my place to look. I just had to motivate myself to go ahead and *do* it."

How can you motivate yourself to get the job done? One way is to make a sketch of where you want things to go, how you want the place to look. A second motivator is a list of all the things that need to be done. Cross things off as you go along. Reward yourself in small ways when you make progress!

Third, look for new ideas until you're satisfied. Most enthusiastic home decorators love to talk about furniture, fabrics, wall coverings, furnishings, and inexpensive ways to pull off these desired changes.

You can also inspire yourself by looking through home-decorating magazines for photographs of rooms that match your taste.

- *Get professional advice.* If you can afford it, hire a decorator, designer, landscape designer, or architect to provide consultation on an hourly or daily basis. Make it clear from the start that you only want consultation, rather than a complete design scheme and rendering (much more expensive!). An experienced professional can give you many new, creative ideas, as well as suggest alternative sources and solutions.

■ *Hire a professional to do everything.* This is the luxury approach. Be sure you know your budget before you commit yourself to this one! Assume that the costs *will* overrun your original estimate! Make sure you can describe clearly how you would like your home to look and what your needs are in terms of living and entertaining. Clip photographs of interiors so the designer has a *visual* image of what appeals to your tastes. If the person you hire is quick to advise without thoroughly exploring your goals, you're probably with the wrong person. Their task is to build on *your* fantasies, not their own.

Strategies for Buying a Home

Maybe an apartment isn't adequate for your needs right now. If you think it's time to buy a house, you aren't alone. In recent years, the largest group of buyers of new housing have been single women! For many men and women who are looking for a sound investment as well as a comfortable living space and a sense of permanence, the advantages outweigh the disadvantages.

Here are some of both:

Advantages:

■ Your property is likely to increase in value.
■ You have many tax advantages when you own a home.
■ You have a stable form of collateral should you need to borrow money.

- The place is totally your own: you can make almost any renovations or improvements you like.
- If you buy property, you have opportunities to do landscaping and gardening.
- You may feel more a *part* of the neighborhood or community as a homeowner.
- If you are moving to a larger home, you have more space for business, entertainment, pets, children, and guests.

Disadvantages:

- You will need a substantial amount of money for the down payment and settlement costs and to make your place livable.
- You are solely responsible for maintenance and upkeep (except for condos and co-ops).
- Resale may be difficult in some parts of the country so it can be harder to move, a consideration if the freedom to relocate is important to you.
- If you want to make a career change or go back to school, owning a home could be more of a burden than an asset.

Choosing a Home

If you have decided that you want to buy, it's a good idea to make a priority list. This list will help you when you start looking.

For example, here are some considerations to keep in mind:

- City, suburbs, or country? Think about where you feel most comfortable and what activities you enjoy. If urban life is appealing, you may feel bored and out-of-it in a suburb where your neighbors are mostly couples and families. On the other hand, if you like lawns and gardens and a more subdued lifestyle, then a suburban setting may be just right for you.

■ Who are your neighbors? In a condo, co-op, or urban environment such as an apartment or town house, you'll undoubtedly be around more single people. If this is what you want, keep that in mind.

■ Are services and stores convenient? When you're looking at a new neighborhood, go back *without* the realtor to talk to potential neighbors, drive around, and check out public places and shopping areas.

■ Do you expect to spend a lot of time fixing up your new house? Be realistic about the time and costs involved. If you have never done home repair, talk to some people who have—especially on your type of dwelling.

■ How much time will you actually spend at home? Again, be realistic. If you are a salesperson on the road all the time, having a one-acre yard may be all trouble and little pleasure.

■ Pets? If you are renting or will belong to a condo or co-op association, find out their policy on pets.

■ Does the home you are about to rent or buy feel right? If not, keep looking. Cosmetic changes and minor renovation can help, but your *basic* feel about your new home should be very positive.

■ Is it structurally sound? Almost anyone who has house-buying experience will recommend that you have the house inspected by a structural engineer or architect *before* making an offer. If the engineer tells you that a roof will need replacing or a chimney needs repair, that's a bargaining chip in your negotiations with the owner. Of course, a serious structural problem is a good reason not to make any offer at all.

■ Before any papers are drawn up, bring in a lawyer with real estate expertise. A lawyer's advice could save you thousands of dollars and many hours of aggravation.

Moving In

"For some reason, this move was very difficult," said Katya, a year after she moved to her new condo. Looking back, she observed a number of things she would have done differently:

> I would have taken a full week's vacation then, instead of trying to get everything done in two days. Also, I think I should have closed on the house a month before I moved in. That would have given me at least a month's head start on the repainting and furnishing. As it was, everything worked out, but it was several months before I had things the way I wanted them and began to really feel comfortable.

As Katya discovered, moving is stressful, especially when you're trying to work at your job, arrange financing, get to closing, and look after the multitude of details that always seem to come up at these times. In addition, there's all the stress of leaving a familiar place.

To give yourself a helping hand, try to prepare in advance for this transition by making things easier for yourself. Here are some suggestions:

- If possible, get fix-ups done *before* you move in. If you can afford to, take possession a full month before you move. Strive to finish wallpapering and painting before carpeting and furniture go in.

- Try to take some days off from work before and after you move. Use those extra days to get books put away, organize the kitchen, hang pictures, and rearrange furniture. Then when you go back to work, your new home will *feel* like home.

- Try to meet some of your neighbors as soon as possible. In a neighborhood of families, the single person can remain an unknown entity for a long time. People are curious about you when you *first* move in. Satisfy their curiosity soon. Chances are you'll make some new friends.

- Find out about neighborhood activities and block parties. Make a point of joining in and helping out *the first time* you have a chance. (Whether you volunteer again will depend on how much you liked helping out the first time.)

Sharing with a Housemate

You don't have to live alone if you don't want to.

To be successful in selecting a housemate, you have to set up your criteria first. Decide *how* you would like to share your life with that other person, then interview carefully. Are you looking for someone who will *become* your friend and companion? Or a boarder who will primarily help share the cost of your home? Your search for a housemate will be most successful if you know what you're looking for.

For best results, keep the lease or mortgage and title *exclusively* in your own name. That way, you retain the final word in case of a dispute. Draw up a separate lease or sublease with your housemate for rent and maintenance costs, utilities, increases in rent or taxes, and all other shared costs.

THINGS TO THINK ABOUT BEFORE YOU CHOOSE A HOUSEMATE

Decide what should be your private areas and what rooms you will share in common. Have a clear plan for sharing all costs.

Then ask yourself:

- Will you take someone with children or pets?
- Any age requirements?
- Must your housemate (or housemates) be the same sex as you?
- Is smoking an issue?
- Are those with certain types of lifestyles preferred or excluded?

WHEN YOU INTERVIEW...

- Ask questions covering every possible issue and be satisfied about everything you need to know *before* you invite the person to move in.
- Let the person know that your agreement will be in writing and will include financial commitments, agreements about moving out or selling, and a method for resolving disputes—legal and otherwise. Have an attorney draw up your lease and agreement.
- Anticipate that unthought-of issues will arise afterward, and make sure that you have a method for working these out. (This is very important!)

TOPICS TO DISCUSS

Following are some topics that I recommend discussing during an interview. You may want to add your own questions to this list. Remember, you may be living with this person for a long time.

- Friendship. Is your prospective housemate looking for you to be a companion—or does he/she expect to have the status of a renter?
- Finances. Find out where the person is employed. Check out his/her credit in order to determine whether he or she can meet monthly payments. What other

commitments does your prospect have: alimony or child support? School tuition or loans? Large car payments or high insurance? You may wish to obtain information from a credit investigation agency.

- Smoking habits. If this is an issue for you, it must be discussed. Will the person agree to house rules about smoking? If you are a smoker and the other person is not, find out whether he or she will tolerate *your* smoking.

- Kitchen use. Talk about mealtimes. Do you expect to eat/cook together? What about entertaining and cleaning up. Decide whether you will choose and buy your food jointly or individually. Find out if the other person has special dietary needs and if this poses any problem.

- Telephones. Will you have separate lines or one line? (I highly recommend separate.) How are installation and monthly costs handled? Will the other person have an answering machine, or expect you to answer when he or she is out?

- Parties. Do you and your prospective housemate expect to have frequent parties? Are there any issues here for you to consider?

- Heating and air conditioning. Discuss this. If you like the house a cool 65 degrees, you probably won't be comfortable with someone who needs it at 78 and is inflexible.

- Neatness. What are *your* requirements? What are the other person's? It is essential to figure if there is a problem here. In the final stages of making your decision, try to see each other's present living spaces. You'll quickly know if you're compatible.

- Children? If the other person has children, will they be living with you full time or part time? Do they have any special problems that could affect you? Is there enough room for everyone to be comfortable? What is the visiting schedule? Is it likely to change? If the other person is trying for custody, could this alter your arrangement?

■ Pets? Is the other person allergic to your cats or dogs? Do they expect to bring their own pets into the house?

■ What will be the arrangement when one person has an overnight guest? When out-of-town friends and family visit?

■ Whose furniture goes where?

■ Will you share yard work and other household chores such as cleaning and minor maintenance? Or will you share the cost of someone to do this for you?

Before making your decision, make sure you have a *process* for discussing issues that are sure to arise. You can expect a few surprises—so can the other person. But as long as you interview carefully and you have an agreed-upon *method* of airing grievances and working out issues, you can usually resolve conflicts. Don't get involved with someone about whom you have initial doubts.

Chapter 36

Security

Lisa lives in a city neighborhood that's on the mend. But it's still borderline, and Lisa is afraid to go out at night.

"It's fine if there are a lot of people on the street," she says, "but I hate to walk here alone. If I'm coming home by myself, I take a cab. I try to get the driver to wait until I get in the door."

"Once I'm in the house I'm okay—usually," she adds. "But I worry if I hear noises. Crazy as it may seem, I even keep a can of Mace next to my bed."

Safety Features

Do you feel safe walking home as a single person at night? Are you secure alone (or with your children) in your own house or apartment? If you take proper precautions, yet still don't feel secure, here are some added security measures you can take:

■ Get to know your neighbors. Police agree that for people living on their own, knowing your neighbors is better than almost any security system money can buy. Feed the neighbors' cats or water their plants while they are away—and let them do the same for you. By trading off some chores with your neighbor, you will have someone to watch the house or apartment while you're away, and you'll be more aware of each other's schedules.

■ Get a dog. A good watchdog will scare off most intruders. The *silence* is also reassuring. Just having a dog in your home that's *not* barking tells you there's no cause for alarm and gives you an added feeling of security. Some training is essential. You're better off if the dog sleeps in the front hall, where it can actually scare someone away, rather than at the foot of your bed.

While small dogs like Yorkies, Chihuahuas, and toy poodles are preferred by many apartment owners, they tend to yap a lot. If a dog is going to be kept at home alone, it is best to buy a mature, well-trained, larger dog that is four or five years old—such as a golden or Labrador retriever or a spaniel. Males should be castrated, and females are preferable to males, since they are less territorial. It is advisable to consult a veterinarian before you decide which kind of dog you want to keep.

Also, count the days you are likely to be away from home. Those are all days when the dog must be kenneled or cared for by a neighbor. But if you are a natural dog-lover who likes to spend time at home, a canine security system may be just what you need.

■ Organize a neighborhood watch. "To be frank, I chose the block I live in because it has a guard," says Sherry, who lives on the Upper West Side of Manhattan. "He's on duty from six o'clock until two A.M. every night. That means I can come home without being afraid. It makes a difference."

Many towns already have a "neighborhood watch" system organized and run by volunteers. If yours doesn't, why not organize a program? Chances are, if you are concerned about crime in your neighborhood, so are others. It should be easy to rally support! It may even be yet another way to meet people.

■ Find a housemate. "Ever since I was a little girl, I've hated being all alone in the house," Ellie told me. A high school teacher with a house in the suburbs, she found that the fear was hard to conquer. She began looking for a housemate.

"A teacher friend of mine, Janet, was complaining about how hard it was for her to find a reasonable place to live. I suddenly thought to myself, This is ridiculous. I'd *love* to have someone else in the house and Janet is the perfect person."

Ellie and Janet decided on the living arrangements, drew up some brief agreements, and Janet moved in a few weeks later.

"I'm enjoying having another person in the house," says Ellie. "And I feel so much safer."

Is a Move in Order?

Ralph had several thousand dollars' worth of stereo and camera equipment stolen from his condominium while he was on vacation. "I changed every lock on the place and installed an alarm system. But I still don't feel safe. I started looking over my shoulder every time I came home. I thought about buying a gun. *That's* when it hit me that maybe it was time to move."

If your life has become uncomfortable like Ralph's, it may be time for you to consider a move to a safer neighborhood.

Chapter 37

Finances

For the single person, finances are as personal an item as your lifestyle in general. If you're living alone, you have complete control over your budget. You earn the salary, you decide how much to spend on food, clothing, and entertainment, and you decide what to put away for the future. In addition, you have to insure yourself so the lifestyle you enjoy will be protected if your health fails or you are unable to work for any reason.

Financially, the single person may feel particularly vulnerable when a marriage or relationship has recently ended. Sometimes, it was the *other* person who handled the finances, insurance, and investments. If this is your situation, you may lack expertise. (This would also be the case if you've recently moved away from your parents and *they* handled the bulk of the financial arrangements.)

It's not uncommon to meet someone divorced or recently separated who just doesn't have a realistic idea of his or her *new* budget. The picture has changed, but the person still isn't quite sure what that picture is. The danger is that the person begins single life by overspending, and it may take a long time to get caught up again.

The other difficult aspect for almost any single person is planning for your future. Retirement may seem a long way off, and if you have a good steady income, no spouse, and no dependents, you may move right into a lifestyle that's very comfortable—and naturally you want to stay there. The tendency is to wait a few years before you start putting some money away toward retirement.

Special Concerns

What are the financial concerns that should be most important to you?

Perhaps the best way to *begin* to answer that question is with a few what-if's. For example . . .

■ *What if* you got sick tomorrow and couldn't work for the next six months? Could you pay your monthly bills? Could you meet doctor bills and hospital expenses?

■ *What if* you really want to retire at age sixty-five (or earlier), without any financial worries? Will you have enough money to continue a lifestyle you like?

■ *What if* you lose your job? Do you have enough in savings to get by until you find another job? Could you get by if you were out of work for six months?

These are matters we must all consider if we're being prudent. But once you've asked the questions . . . then what? The best policy, of course, is to take precautions so you will be prepared.

How about day-to-day finances? After all, just getting by, month after month, can seem like a challenge.

Recently, I discussed this issue with Bob Madigan, an expert on financial matters for Westwood One/NBC Talknet. Madigan, along with Lawrence Kasoff, is also the coauthor of *The First-Time Investor* (Prentice Hall, 1986).

"Don't be frightened by finances," Madigan advises. "Look at everything you're doing as an investment in yourself. Then plan that investment, so you will have the money to spend when you need it."

Rules Worth Gold

Madigan doesn't like to talk about a *budget*. Instead, he calls it a *spending plan*—because you're planning how to *spend* money on yourself. "Some of it you will spend now, and some later," says Madigan. "But it's still all yours."

For a single person, the hardest spending to think about is the kind that's thirty or forty years away. Investing in that far-off time requires some discipline. But many single people tell me they wish they had started to save earlier. As one single woman in her late thirties said to me, "I'm just beginning to look at a retirement plan—and I wish I'd thought about my investments a little earlier. It would be easier for me now if I'd started saving in my twenties."

So it's important to look at your present spending plan, and to begin fitting investment into it—along with all the current expenditures. To do that, you have to figure out where it goes, what is essential, and what you might cut from your current spending plan to ensure your future financial worth.

Insurance

Madigan observes that single people should pay special attention to their coverage in *disability insurance* and *health insurance*. Life insurance, on the other hand, is really only essential to someone who has a family. If you have dependents, of course, you will definitely need adequate life insurance. But for single people without dependents, life insurance really isn't necessary.

Disability insurance is absolutely essential. If you're a single person living alone and you have to stop working for any reason—where will you find an income? You probably don't want to depend on your parents, even if they *could* support you at a time like that. Though you may have a few investments, those should be long-range funds, and you'll want to protect them as much as possible.

The only answer is disability insurance. I've talked to a number of singles who assume that they have enough disability coverage from their employer or from their state insurance. But often these plans are minimal and inadequate. The only way to really figure it out is to add up what you spend every month, then look at the disability coverage you already have to find out whether it will take care of you.

If it won't, shop for a policy.

DISABILITY INSURANCE ADVICE

Madigan points out that the price of disability insurance is *very* high if it begins from the first day of illness. It's much more economical to have some just-in-case savings that will cover you during the first few months.

If your illness keeps you off the job longer than that, your disability insurance should pay enough every month to meet all your expenses.

"I tell people to have enough ready cash to support them for at least the first three months," says Madigan, "and you should have a disability plan that kicks in after that."

1. *Ready cash.* Keep the three months' worth of take-home pay in a liquid account. In case anything happens to you, you have instant access to this money to replace your lost salary.

Don't give in to the temptation to use this money for anything else. Just because it's liquid doesn't mean it's available. Keep this three-month cushion intact!

2. *Shopping for disability insurance.* If your employer does not provide disability insurance, shop around and compare prices. Be sure to compare apples to apples. If you follow Madigan's advice and cover yourself for the first three months, then you want to compare plans that begin in the fourth month of the disability. If the premiums seem very high, you might want to consider how you could cut back your monthly expenses if you were seriously ill. Transportation, entertainment, and casual shopping will be minimal if you're housebound. On the other hand, you might have to pay for extras like food delivery or house-cleaning— so be realistic. I'm sure none of us likes to think very much about being disabled, but you have a responsibility to *yourself* to prepare for that now. No one can do it for you.

HEALTH INSURANCE

In the area of health insurance, single people sometimes get caught short when they are without a spouse who either took care of that insurance or had a comprehensive plan through his or her employer.

Working out your insurance may seem like just another burden. But health insurance is essential—no one should be without it at any time—and if you aren't adequately covered, the consequences could be very serious. If you're just getting used to living on your own, you *don't* want the additional financial burden of health costs.

Review the coverage you now have. You should be insured for hospitalization and catastrophic illness. If the insurance is handled by your employer, find someone in your company who can answer your questions—or go directly to the insurer.

If your current coverage is not enough, talk to your employer first about additional benefits. Being on a group plan gives you substantially reduced rates. You don't want to go shopping for other plans if you don't have to. (If you are self-employed, you may be able to get group-plan rates through a professional organization that you already belong to, or one that you can join.)

When shopping for insurance, remember—the higher the deductible, the lower the monthly premium. So you are much better off if you can put some ready cash in savings rather than pay monthly for the lower deductible. Have the exact figures and options explained to you by the company's representative or your own insurance agent. Also read the policy thoroughly and get whatever advice you need to make an informed decision about your coverage.

For single people, it's especially helpful to know

your insurance agent and to know where you can reach him or her in case of an emergency. While your friends may support you in many ways when you're sick or homebound, you can't expect them to do paperwork for you or research a health claim. A good agent can answer your questions quickly and help get prompt response to your claims. If your insurance comes through your company, find the individual in your company who knows the most about dealing with your insurer.

LIFE INSURANCE

As mentioned, a single person only needs life insurance if you have someone depending on your income or if you hold a mortgage. For these situations, purchase term, not whole, life insurance.

A Spending Plan

Many couples have difficulties with finances. Often, one spouse loves to spend, while the other wants to save and prepare for the future. Their financial decisions are often a compromise.

Single people, on the other hand, have neither the benefits nor the drawbacks of such compromises. If you're a free-spender living on your own, no one says to you, "Hey, how come your MasterCard looks like the national debt this month?" If you tend to be cautious, on the other hand, there's no one but yourself to say, "Go have a big night—you *deserve* it!"

So we really have to get the dialogue going ourselves. You know your own tendencies—free-spender, saver, or somewhere in the middle—and can figure out ways to balance those tendencies. Then the trick is to get on a spending plan that holds you to a month-by-month pattern. The nice thing is, if you stick to that spending plan and play by your own rules, you don't have to worry about debating with yourself about every little purchase or entertainment item.

Dennis, a hotel manager in his early thirties, told me, "It was very, very easy for me to spend money when I started in this business. I seemed to be making more every year. Then my salary increases leveled off, and suddenly I found myself wondering, Where's it all going?"

Dennis found that getting control of his finances was "mostly psychological."

> I worked it out so I never saw a whole paycheck. My bank has an automatic payment system. So I deposited my entire check, took out a fixed amount as pocket money. All my bills were paid every month by the bank. Once I had it set up, it worked because I never saw the money that wasn't *supposed* to be pocket money. I spend less on trivia, but that's a pretty small sacrifice.

Divide Your Take-Home Pay

Of course the details of your own financial plan will depend on your individual needs and income. But as Bob Madigan emphasizes, the most important thing to remember is—*divide up your take-home pay.* Before you spend it, have a plan for putting aside certain percentages for fixed expenses and investments. And stick to that plan! You will go a long way toward ensuring your financial future.

Following are guidelines for spending that, according to financial planners, apply to almost everyone:

■ *Housing.* No more than 25 to 30 percent of your take-home pay should go to housing. That includes rent or mortgage, taxes, insurance, and condo fees (if any). In determining whether you are eligible to take out a mortgage, most banks use 30 percent of income as the top figure.

But your single-person budget might not allow you to buy that gem of real estate that you *know* will be a good investment. What should you do in that case?

Most financial planners recommend that you not exceed the 30 percent level, even if the investment side looks very good. But why not plan on renting part of it or sharing with a housemate? Before you buy, figure out what you will have to put into the property to make it suitable for a renter. You can offer a short-term lease, and the renter will help you stay within your budget until your income reaches a level where you can meet payments.

Also, if you are attracted to a house primarily as an investment, keep in mind that other kinds of investments could take less of your income and make more sense at this time. As a rule of thumb, says Madigan, "If you can rent for half of what your total monthly house payment would be if you were purchasing, then it might not make much sense to buy."

■ *Food.* An average family should not be spending more than 25 percent of take-home pay on food—so you, as a single person, can spend a lot less if you're careful. It's harder to overspend at the supermarket than it is to overspend at high-priced restaurants. If you're over the 15-to-20-percent line on food, plan on more meals at home and go to more modestly priced restaurants when you eat out.

■ *Savings and Investments.* When it comes to long-term savings, too many single people count on a future relationship that will involve someone who will pro-

319 SURVIVAL STRATEGIES 319

vide all the security they need. This is too risky. *You* have to provide for *you*—and if you later meet someone who's in great shape financially, so much the better.

Ideally, you should put about 15 percent of your take-home pay into savings and investments every month. Some of the money can go into an FDIC-insured savings account; some into low-risk investments; some into medium- or high-risk investments. The key is to leave the money in and let it earn compound interest. This is your long-term savings. If you leave it alone it will grow and do wonders for you later on.

- *Credit Cards.* As noted, this is a battleground for many couples. The single person, on the other hand, has no one to say, "WHAT'S THIS?" when the bill comes in at the end of the month. If you don't have an inner voice that says STOP!, you may have to alter your credit-card policy drastically.

Bob Madigan says *no more than 10 percent of your earnings should go to credit-card and revolving accounts.* He strongly recommends that credit-card expenditures not exceed what you can pay when the bill comes.

- *Clothing.* About 5 percent of take-home pay.

- *Which all adds up to . . .* 85 percent or less of your income! That leaves 15 percent for your automobile, entertainment, vacations, insurance, Christmas gifts, and everything else not included above.

These are general guidelines, but many single people have found them to be extremely valuable. After all, you don't want to argue with *yourself* every time you make a purchase or pay a bill—but you do need a way to balance out your natural tendencies. If you follow the rules of this spending plan, you can feel secure that you are taking care of yourself.

Investment Plans

In a marriage or relationship, invariably one person or the other becomes the *ex officio* investment specialist. Both might know where their money is being invested, but usually one person is more responsible for keeping track of interest rates, tax breaks, and investment opportunities.

As a single person, you have no option but to become the investment specialist for yourself. However, that doesn't mean you have to be an *expert*. You can seek out experts and ask their advice. You can interview financial planners and investment counselors to find out what they can do for you, and on what terms. And you can stay alert to new investment possibilities by talking to friends, parents, or colleagues about trends or opportunities that they see.

If you don't have any background in investments, I would recommend taking an adult education course that will introduce you to the fundamentals. Here, you can get some of your basic questions answered. Often these courses are taught by financial planners who are promoting their services as well as teaching the basics. If you like the teacher, that person might help you get started.

However, always find out in advance *how* a planner charges for his or her services. You probably want someone who charges a flat fee. You will save money in the long run, because the planner will teach you how to make decisions on your own. (Planners who charge *no fee* make their money by getting you to invest in vehicles that specifically make commissions for *them*, such as mutual funds, stocks, IRA's and bonds. Thus they do not give objective advice, so be careful.)

Many excellent night-school courses in financial planning are available. Check community colleges, high school adult education programs, and institutions like the Learning Annex. Even in a beginner's course in household finance, you can learn everything from the basics of balancing a checkbook to the fundamentals of sound investing.

Accept the Challenge

I have already mentioned the financial shock that single people often experience when they are ending a marriage or coming out of a relationship. Lifestyles can change drastically. Your household budget may be cut by more than half. Expenses in a divorce settlement can run sky-high, and these expenses hit just as you're trying to resettle yourself, get over the relationship, and find out what you have to live on.

At a time like this, the rule of thumb is *to be as conservative as possible* in your spending until some months have gone by and you find out what's actually involved in living alone and taking care of your own needs.

Norma came from a wealthy family and married a mortgage broker. Up to and through the time of her divorce, she held a part-time job as the curator of an art museum. Because she and her husband could both live off his income, her own salary was really discretionary income that she spent largely on household and personal items. She had a credit card in her own name, but her husband customarily paid off the monthly balance.

When she and her husband were divorced, Norma quickly made an adjustment in her lifestyle. She moved to a small apartment and cut back on her spending. However, she decided to use the credit card to furnish her new apartment. In just one month, she added charges up to the limit of $5,000.

She could meet the minimum payment, but that was all. Month after month, the high finance charge kept taking away her savings. It wasn't until she changed jobs and significantly increased her income that she finally paid off the balance. After that, she never put more on the credit card than she could pay off in a single month.

"When I made the last payment on that credit card, I finally felt totally in control of my new life," said Norma. "It was as if some blot from the past had been erased and I could start over again. Ever since then, I've been very careful with my budget. My income is really mine, and I enjoy watching where it goes."

Look for the Challenge

One of the worst images that single people sometimes have is that of being alone and penniless. (In fact, this fear sometimes keeps people in relationships that otherwise don't work!) When you get control over your own financial destiny, that fear goes away.

If you understand your situation and apply a few basic rules—plus a little trial and error—you will discover another aspect of your life to which you can apply the gift of choice! It is indeed a challenge, but anyone who can hold a job and run a household is certainly capable of meeting that challenge.

Afterword

Shaping the Single Life

Throughout this book, I have asked you many times to take inventories of your attitudes. It's very important to discover how you look at the world and to find out what you really want from life so that you can achieve a clearer understanding of your goals.

I have also presented many strategies and practical steps for *getting* what you want. The more tools for living that you have at your command, the more you can expect to achieve satisfaction and fulfillment.

But above all, I have emphasized a message that I believe is very important for every person who is living single: *Yes, you do have power over your life!*

You can shape, design, and mold your life. You have the power to set the pattern for days and nights, weeks and weekends. You can use strategies to extend and enrich your social life. You can find ways to enjoy being alone without being lonely. If it's romance you want, you can explore new ways to seek relationships—and to nurture a relationship that seems fulfilling to you.

You command the ability to begin friendships, sustain them, and make them grow stronger. You have the survival skills to manage all the details of running a household, whether you are living alone, caring for children, or looking out for others. Although there are many demands on your time and energy, you can manage your financial and professional affairs, plan your future, ensure health care and continued income in case of a medical problem, provide for your retirement, and look out for your own security.

If you share a household with others, you have the ability to care for the people who depend on you and to see that their needs are met as well as your own. If you are living by yourself, you can balance the time you spend alone and the time you spend with others. You have the power to balance work time and play time, obligations and entertainments.

Whether or not a long-term relationship is in the cards for you, you can plan your future with confidence that you can enjoy life on your own. Plan on making your own home comfortable and *right* for you. Plan on spending many good times with people whom you enjoy. And plan on the rewards of discovering rich solitude.

Always keep in mind that you have the option of growing *out* of some relationships and *into* others, and you can become more skilled in your choosing.

You cannot control the future, but you *can* set directions for yourself. And if you are committed to your goals, you are likely to see many of your dreams become a reality.

It is my hope that you will recognize this power and use it to the fullest, every day. Take advantage of the flexibility and the possibilities at your command to design your attitudes and shape a healthy, successful, and fulfilling life.

Shaping

At the beginning of this book, I described *Kate*, a twenty-eight-year-old woman who was recently divorced. When Kate first came to see me, she said she was lonely. She was unhappy with single life. She felt stuck. She wanted to know where she should be going in her friendships and relationships. She wanted help!

Many of the strategies in this book resemble those that Kate used in designing single life for herself. To put these strategies into action, she had to change her attitude about her situation. She ceased to become a victim of loneliness and confusion. She gained mastery over her own self-esteem so that, finally, she could say, "I *like* myself—and I'm going to shape my life in the way that's right for *me*."

For *Nina*, shaping single life meant understanding the importance of relationships: "I had to accept the fact that the development of a relationship has its own timing. I realize that I am really and truly not ready for commitment. I've had to accept how that feels and come to grips with it, and make it work for me."

For *Claudia*, single life has offered the opportunity to shape her career and increase her self-confidence.

Marty discovered that he was much happier with single life when he reshaped his attitude so he was not always waiting for the right woman to come along: "I have no intention of being married. I wouldn't rule it out, but I just don't see the advantages right now. I like to meet people. I like the freedom to come and go. There are just too many things I would have to give up if I were married."

For *Dorothy*, shaping her single life simply meant surrounding herself with energetic people.

Choosing for Yourself

How will you shape your own single life? The choice is yours. In addition to the strategies that I have described in this book, you have great resources at your command—your own abilities, your friends, your career, your romantic interests, and above all, your desire to be successful at what you do. If you can enjoy living the good single life, that is the greatest sign of your success!

At the beginning of this book, I told you that I definitely have enjoyed the single life. Living single has allowed me to build my career and develop friendships I might never have had otherwise.

On the other hand, designing my own single life did not come automatically to me any more than it might to you. It was an exercise in trial and error—sometimes frustrating, other times exhilarating, and still other times calm and uneventful.

I believe that the skills you develop as a single person are not restricted to the art of living single. Nor, as you may have guessed, is this book *just* about singles. The art of living single is really the art of living . . . *period! Now* is the time to shape that art to your tastes—and *now* is the time to make it work for you!

Index